THE MURAL BOOK
A PRACTICAL GUIDE FOR EDUCATORS

JANET BRAUN-REINITZ AND ROCHELLE SHICOFF

ISBN 1-56290-241-5
Printed in Hong Kong

TO ALL MURAL MAKERS, PAST, PRESENT, AND FUTURE

1a-b. East New York Women's Wall, Braun-Reinitz and Shicoff

TABLE OF CONTENTS

INTRODUCTION

For more than twenty years, we have been passionately involved in mural-making, committed to collaboration and community participation and the *pizzazz* of painting in public.

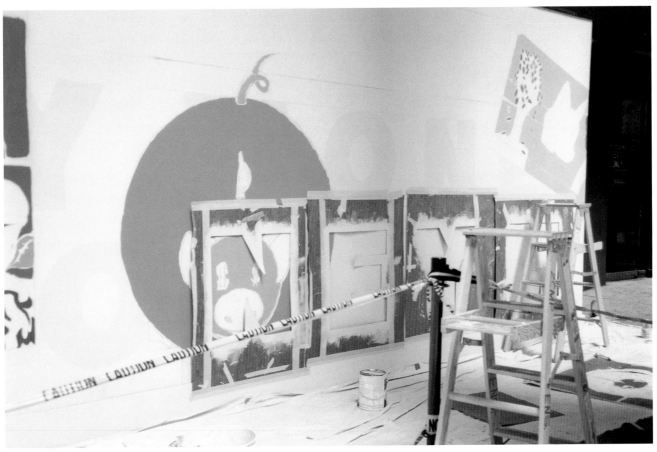

2. Acrylic paint on plywood, high school (detail)

Murals are large works of wall art created for a particular place with a specific theme that is relevant to the site. Indoors or outdoors, murals are intended to be permanent and viewed by a large audience. Through the centuries, muralists have created an amazing array of art on walls, from dining rooms in Pompeii to the Sistine Chapel, from Egyptian tombs to American Post Offices, from Algeria to Turkey, Mexico City, and Milwaukee.

The size and challenge of making a mural is one of its most attractive and energizing features. Because the very word "mural" connotes big, some educators have shied away from what seems too daunting an enterprise for the school setting. We disagree. Our process, tailored for the classroom, is an appropriate and rich visual arts experience based on teaching collaboration, skill-building, and sequential learning. In fact, this book was written in response to the many inquiries, over the years, from classroom and art teachers eager to make murals with their students.

You do not have to be an artist to use this book successfully. The practices we have developed and present here are designed to guide you through the entire experience of teaching mural-making from start to finish. Each chapter will take you through the process sequentially, step-by-step for reference and clarity. We have selected three different types of murals that are appropriate for kindergarten through grade twelve classroom use; the painted mural, the paper collage mural, and the fabric mural.

By using this book, you and your class will become part of the larger collaboration of teachers, students, and artists who make murals. Welcome.

In the later chapters of the book, you will see the following symbol: ·ᐁ·

This icon refers you to other sections of the book where the subject is discussed in more detail.

CHAPTER ONE

THINKING BIG, STARTING SMALL: PROPOSING AND PLANNING

THE FIRST STEPS in any project, the *getting going*, often seem the most difficult. Fear Not.

3. Acrylic paint on masonite, 4th grade

You are already involved in numerous instructional activities essential for creating a class mural project. You think ahead and pre-plan, communicate and share ideas with students and colleagues, organize lessons in a step-by-step method and identify school personnel who are integral to specific long-range planning. With your skills and the clearly defined steps of proposing and planning in this chapter, you are on your way to a comfortable and successful beginning.

IDENTIFYING GOALS

The first step begins with thinking about what YOU want to accomplish through this project.

Make a list of your goals.

- What are your goals as a teacher?
- What are your goals for your students?
- Goals may include:
  - reinforcing other areas of the curriculum
  - teaching visual arts curriculum
  - developing learning through collaboration
  - strengthening habits of sequential learning
- What are your goals for the larger school community?
  - beautifying the school
  - demonstrating the high quality of student work

CHOOSING THE MEDIUM

For your class's age, needs, and skills, what is the most appropriate medium—paint, paper, fabric?

There are four basic support choices—walls, wood panels (Chapter 4), foam core (Chapter 9), or felt fabric (Chapter 10).

- For interior surfaces, you can use walls, wood panels, foam core sheets, or felt fabric.
- For exterior surfaces, you can only use walls or wood panels, no paper or fabric.

4. Fabric, 4th/5th grade

CHOOSING A SITE

A mural is public, large-scale, site specific, and attracts a large audience. The choice of location will determine much about the scope of the project.

With a yard stick or tape measure, pencil and paper, identify and measure two or three possible sites. Beyond the hallway walls, you might consider doors, gymnasium, auditorium, cafeteria, or exterior walls and doors. Keep your options open. Do not make the common mistake of *falling in love* with one space as the perfect site.

5. Acrylic paint on brick, 5th grade (detail)

PROPOSING

Make an appointment with the principal. Be prepared to answer some typically asked questions:

- Where is the mural going to be installed?
- What is the theme and medium?
- How much time will it take?
- How much will it cost?

Take the principal on a tour of the potential sites you have selected. Encourage his/her input in both adding to and narrowing the choices until you both have agreed on a site. Now is the appropriate time for the principal to make an appointment with the custodian for a three-way meeting.

Consult several other members of the school community for various permissions as well as for their expertise, support, and advice. The principal should become an active partner in making the decision to create a public mural in your school. He/she sets the tone for the entire building. The support and ideas of the principal will insure that your mural project will proceed.

Custodians are the only people with the know-how regarding the physical plant, and they will appreciate being included as participants in this preliminary decision-making process.

Art teachers can be valuable resources for your project. Their involvement connects the mural project with what the students are learning in their art curriculum.

With a site selected and the cooperation of the principal, custodian, and art teacher, the initial proposing steps of the mural process are complete.

6. *Acrylic paint on wood door, high school (detail)*

It is our experience that no two custodians greet the news of an impending mural on their walls with the same attitude or enthusiasm. Without their cooperation, your site is not assured. Ask advice on the details of installation strategies.

Invite the art teacher to give specially prepared lessons to the class in color, composing, and painting that are specific to the mural.

PLANNING

As you begin, allow time to assemble materials and plan the installation and the celebration.

Understanding your time commitment and the in-class time commitment for your mural project is one of the essential ingredients for realistic planning.

Each mural session should be at least one hour long for younger children, and one-and-a-half to two hours long for older children. Meet twice a week. For junior and senior high school students, where it is difficult to change schedules, alternatives can include scheduling double periods or working during art classes or in afterschool programs. The medium you select for your mural will determine the number of hours it will take. Typically, the painted mural takes 24 to 32 hours, the paper mural 10 hours, and the fabric mural 12 to 15 hours.

You may have more flexibility in organizing your time than in creating your budget. At the initial stage of your mural planning, it is essential to know how much money is available.

In all cases, whether it is paint, paper, collage, or fabric, it is important to use good quality materials. The cost of supplies for making your mural depends on the medium you select. Specific budgets are listed at the end of the appropriate chapters Four, Nine, and Ten.

If your school cannot pay directly for all of the supplies, there are many other ways to acquire them and help you save money:

- The art department may have brushes and other non-consumable supplies that you can borrow.
- Your colleagues may have fabric and trim scraps, buckets, and cardboard to contribute.
- Parents of your students or members of the Parent Association may have access to discounts at stores.
- Ask hardware stores, stationery stores, and lumber yards to make donations.

You have now completed the proposing and initial planning steps of your mural project.

Your action and enthusiasm will supply the momentum to carry you and your class through this unusual, large-scale, messy, collaborative, and impressive project.

7. Acrylic paint on masonite, high school (detail)

CHAPTER TWO

THE LANGUAGE OF ART: THEORY AND PRACTICE

AS YOUR STUDENTS actually create their mural and you begin conversing with them about their work, you will be considering and analyzing the progress of their efforts. What does it look like? How are all the pieces of this giant puzzle working together? How are the choices of colors helping the viewer's eye move through the mural?

8. *Acrylic paint on plywood,*
   4th grade (detail)

Visual art can be created, looked at, and appreciated without a word being spoken. But, in order to discuss the mural-in-progress, you need words that carry specific meaning to communicate and clarify the students' artistic concepts.

The visual arts have their own unique vocabulary, as do the sciences, sports, music, technology, and the law. Here, the language of the visual arts, the **ELEMENTS** and the **PRINCIPLES** are identified, defined, and applied through the use of a specific mural example at the end of this chapter.

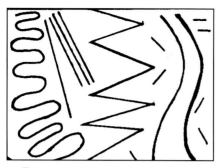

9. Expressive lines

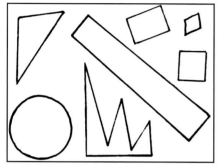

10a. Shapes

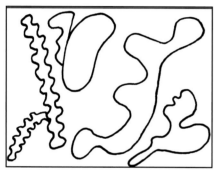

10b. Shapes

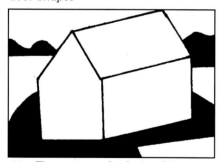

11a. Figure-ground relationship

11b. Positive and negative shapes

ELEMENTS OF ART

The basic ingredients of all visual arts are called the **ELEMENTS—LINE**, **SHAPE**, **FORM**, **SPACE**, **TEXTURE**, and **COLOR**.

LINE. A line is an extended dot, a continuous expressive stroke or mark. It is usually on a two-dimensional surface, has direction, and can be diagonal, horizontal, vertical, bold, delicate, long, short, blurred, or clear while it meanders, twists, hesitates, or rushes.

SHAPE. A shape is a line that meets itself creating an enclosed space. It has only two dimensions and can be curvy, spiky, tiny, slender, bulky, geometric, or free-form.

A shape in a drawing or painting is called the *positive* shape. The surrounding space is called the *negative* shape and is the place where the eye can rest. This fusion is called a **FIGURE-GROUND** relationship with the *positive* as the *figure* and the *negative* as the *ground* (background). Each of these shapes is created by the other and is equally important.

FORM. Form is three-dimensional with height, width, and depth, and is the most important element in sculpture and architecture. Mural-making uses shapes rather than forms.

SPACE. Space in art is either:

- Pictorial—the two-dimensional surface of paper, fabric, or panels, also known as the *picture plane* or
- Actual—only exists in the three-dimensional world (architecture, ceramics, or sculpture).

12. Overlapping

13a. Linear perspective

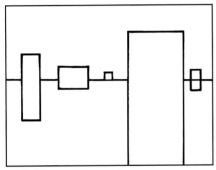

13b. Linear perspective

14. Texture

15. Primary and secondary colors

There are a variety of ways to create the *illusion* of actual space:

- **OVERLAPPING**. One shape covers part of another. It will appear to the eye as if one shape is in front of the other.
- **PERSPECTIVE**. Linear perspective is a system in which all horizontal and parallel lines meet at an invisible vanishing point, creating a foreground, middleground, and background.
  - Large shapes placed in the foreground seem closer than shapes that are smaller and higher on the picture plane.

TEXTURE. Texture is the tactile quality of a surface—soft, pebbly, scratchy, slick. Simulated or implied texture is created by using marks to give the *illusion* of a real surface.

COLOR. Color is a complex element. Scientists understand it as information that impacts on our retina. For artists, color can be used in an expressive and imaginative way. All paintings depend upon color to attract and stimulate viewers. Everyone responds to color both emotionally and intellectually. For painters, colors are categorized in many ways.

- **PRIMARY** colors

  Red, yellow, and blue are the basis for mixing all other colors.

- **SECONDARY** colors

  The secondary colors (orange, violet, and green) are created by mixing two primary colors together (red+yellow=orange, blue+red=violet, and yellow+blue=green).

- **BROWN**

  Three primaries mixed together or three secondaries mixed together make brown.

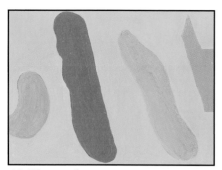

16. Warm colors

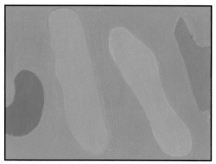

17. Cool colors

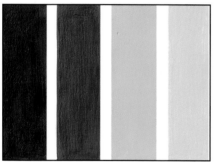

18. Values

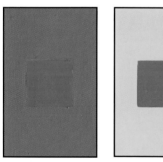

19. Color relationships

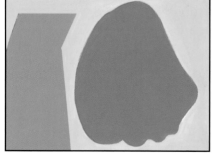

20. Complementary colors

- **WARM** colors.

  Yellow, red, and orange. They remind us of sun, fire, and heat, and we generally perceive them as *advancing*.

- **COOL** colors.

  Blue, green, and violet. These remind us of grass, water, and sky, and usually *recede*.

- **VALUE.**

  Value refers to the light and dark qualities of a color as expressed in **TINTS** and **SHADES**.

- **TINTS.**

  Tints are created when white is added to a color (red+white=pink).

- **SHADES.**

  Shades are created when black is added to a color (red+black=maroon).

COLOR RELATIONSHIPS:

The placement of colors in relationship to each other determines our perception of them. For example, the same red will seem to be altered when placed on different color grounds. The red can appear to recede or advance, look quiet or bold, small or large, depending on its neighboring colors.

Colors that are opposite each other on the color wheel; i.e. red and green, blue and orange, yellow and purple, are called **COMPLEMENTARY COLORS**. When a pair is used together, they create a vivid contrast and extra emphasis.

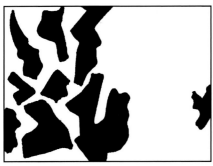

21. Emphasis

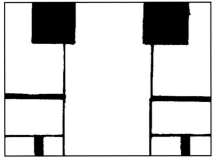

22. Symmetrical balance

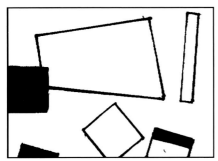

23a. Asymmetrical balance

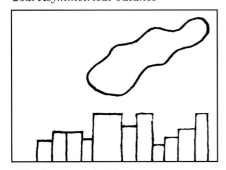

23b. Asymmetrical balance

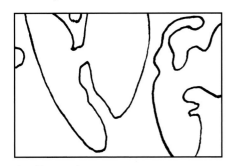

24. Proportion

PRINCIPLES OF ART

The **PRINCIPLES** of art—**EMPHASIS**, **BALANCE**, **PROPORTION**, **RHYTHM**, **PATTERN**, **VARIETY**, **CONTRAST**, and **UNITY** are basic guides in successfully organizing a work of art.

EMPHASIS. Emphasis is the center of attention or one dominant area that catches your eye. It is created by:

- placing a large, significant shape near the center
- using unusual combinations of subjects, shapes, textures, and colors
- isolating a shape or subject

BALANCE. Symmetrical or formal balance in artworks is the even distribution of visual weight on both sides of a center. This mirror image can lead to a static composition. Asymmetrical or informal balance still maintains visual stability, but each side is dissimilar in color, shape, or detail. This will usually result in a more active and unique work of art.

Balance can be achieved by:

- repeating small, vividly colored shapes near large, less intense areas
- placing complicated shapes near simpler shapes
- using dark colors near light colors

PROPORTION. Proportion in all artworks is the harmonious relationship of the size of the parts to each other and the whole. Proportion can be of two kinds:

- realistic (what we see in our surroundings)
- overstated or distorted

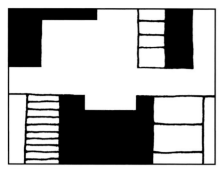

25. Rhythm

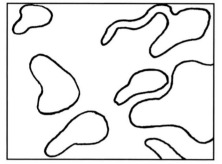

26a. Pattern

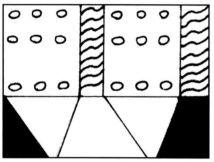

26b. Pattern

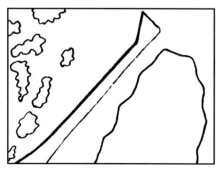

27. Variety and contrast

RHYTHM. Rhythm is created when the art elements are placed throughout an artwork in controlled regular or irregular intervals. This flow or pause directs your eye around the entire work by repeating colors, shapes, or lines.

PATTERN. Pattern is the repetition of similar lines and shapes distributed throughout a composition. Pattern can also be the repetition of the same shapes within an area, such as pineapple skin, leaves, and windows.

VARIETY and **CONTRAST.** Variety and contrast are the essential **PRINCIPLES** for avoiding sameness and monotony. Shapes of different sizes, curved or straight lines, and light and dark colors in unusual placements can create visual surprises.

UNITY. Unity is the result of all the art elements in an artwork working together so that nothing is missing and nothing can be added.

28. Unity, acrylic print on brick, ages 12 to 16 (detail)

COMPOSING. Composing is a pivotal step in artmaking, but it is neither an **ELEMENT** nor a **PRINCIPLE**. Composing is the act of assembling, planning, and organizing all of the elements into a cohesive visual whole where the **ELEMENTS** and **PRINCIPLES** come together in a synthesis.

Are there rules to insure successful composing? The answer is both *no* and *yes*. Each of us has a nonverbal understanding of what looks *right* or *beautiful* that is based on a shared cultural aesthetic. Strict rules do not apply when you are using your intuition and trusting your eyes.

But *yes*, there are approaches rooted in the **PRINCIPLES OF ART** that can be concretely applied to your composing adventure.

Composing is complex. How will you know when you have completed the mural composition? Through trial and error, rearranging, editing, and rethinking, all the images will look and feel right and all the parts will work together. (**UNITY**)

APPROACHES TO COMPOSING A MURAL

In front of you are several large primed panels or walls, paper, or fabric supports. The images, drawings (painted mural), or paper shapes (paper mural) or fabric shapes (fabric mural) are all individual parts of a large puzzle.

- Arbitrarily lay out all of the images on the support.
- Select a drawing, cut paper image, or fabric image that is both large and a focus of the mural narrative. Place it near the center. (**EMPHASIS**)
- If your narrative is a history, an evolution, or any other timeline, it can be composed in a logical sequence, usually from left to right. (**BALANCE**)
- Look for one geometric shape that occurs in different images (circle, rectangle, triangle—i.e. lettuce, sun, balls, tires, heads on figures, which are all circles). Distribute these similar shapes throughout the composition. (**RHYTHM**)
- Look for colors that can be repeated throughout the mural. (**RHYTHM**) Repetition does not necessarily mean that one color is used over and over. A family of colors — yellow/orange, mustard yellow, pale yellow, and yellow/green — can be used. (**RHYTHM**)
- Overlap images to create depth and variety. (**SPACE**)
- Place a cluster of small shapes near a big shape. (**PROPORTION**)

29. Acrylic paint on brick,
ages 9 to 14 (detail)

Although the **ELEMENTS** and **PRINCIPLES** are defined separately, in reality they all interact and are interdependent. We have included the following mural example with questions and answers to help you, and in turn your students, become familiar enough with the application of the **ELEMENTS** and **PRINCIPLES** to use them in a purposeful way.

30. Acrylic paint on plywood, ages 11 to 13

APPLYING THE LANGUAGE OF ART

What color is repeated to help your eye move through the mural?

The strongest repeated color is red, from the shirt shape on the far left to the hair shape, bird shape, sun shape, and across the sun tail down to the shirt shape on the right. Another repeated color is in the yellow family. Look at the right big land shape. Your eye moves to the lettuce land shape and onto the tree land shape on the left. There are also other yellow shapes distributed throughout the mural.

Where are colors used to create emphasis?

The red of the sun shape is definitely one color that says, "Come and look here," as does the purple of the tree shape.

Where do groups of shapes create variety? Contrast? Give specific examples.

On the top right, the groups of patterns in the land shapes and the elongated dark pink curved shape make a visual surprise among the large rectangular land shapes.

How are overlapping and perspective used to organize the pictorial space?

All of the figures and plants are placed on top of large colorful geometric land shapes that cross the whole mural. By using overlapping, the figures and plants appear to be in front of the land shapes. The large figures in the foreground seem closer than the smaller shapes that are higher on the picture plane.

How is asymmetrical balance achieved?

Dark colors have been placed near light colors throughout the mural. On the left, the vertical shapes of the man, woman, and tree are repeated by the vertical groups of patterns on the right (lettuce, carrots, curved lines).

Applying the **ELEMENTS** and **PRINCIPLES** as we have done here will provide solutions for most of your composing questions and allow you to check your intuitive choices.

FIVE EASY PIECES: THEMES · BRAINSTORMING · PICTURE FILE · COLLABORATION · THE SHAPE LESSON

WHETHER YOU ARE a second grade teacher making a paper collage mural for a hallway, a fifth grade teacher planning a multipanel painted mural, or a junior high school teacher creating a fabric mural, the process of making a mural with your class is magic.

31. Acrylic paint on plywood, high school (detail)

In mural-making, a variety of strategies and skills are layered together to create a rich intellectual challenge, a creative hands-on experience, and an impressive finished art work. The process reinforces the educational objectives that you include in many areas of your curriculum—critical thinking, listening skills, sequential learning, and verbal and non-verbal communication.

Through their own experiences with this participatory, personal, and accessible process, students develop a greater appreciation for art and aesthetics, collaborative and problem-solving skills, and the ability to concentrate and work hard.

This chapter explains the sequence of steps that are common to making paper collage, fabric, and painted murals—choosing a theme, brainstorming, creating a picture file, collaborating, and teaching the shape lesson.

THEMES

The teacher selects the broad subject of the mural before the project is introduced to the class. It is usually related to another discipline in the curriculum: science, social studies, history, mathematics, literature, or any combination of these.

What are you trying to identify, communicate, or celebrate?

- You may want to focus on your own environment, a subject that encompasses natural science, local history, and art.

- If your curriculum linkage is Japan, the subject of your mural could be Japanese arts and culture. This leads to other hands-on activities such as papermaking, origami, printmaking, kite making, and writing haiku poetry.

- In the case of sensitive topics such as violence, drugs, sexual politics, environmental issues, health concerns, and historical interpretation, we encourage you to explore them. This is an important opportunity for students to see the effect that art can have and the power of a specific visual image, even if students choose to go in another direction.

32. Acrylic paint on plywood, 4th grade (detail)

33. Fabric, high school (detail)

*34. Acrylic paint on cement,
Hestia Art Collective*

To begin this project, your class needs to agree on a working definition of a mural. This class discussion sets a participatory tone for the entire process.

*35. Acrylic paint on brick,
Braun-Reinitz (detail)*

This newly acquired understanding of murals can now be applied to the specific scope of your class mural.

DEFINING A MURAL

What is a mural?

With your students, make a list on the board of the properties that define a mural:

- large scale

- site specific

- narrative (tells a story)

- seen by a large audience

Explore the students' firsthand experiences with murals:

- Where have you seen a mural? Indoors or outdoors?

- How big was the mural?

- What story did it tell?

- How was the story/theme related to the site?
    - an animal mural at the zoo
    - a "History of the Golden Gate Bridge" mural in San Francisco
    - the "How Machines Work" mural near the science room

Students can use the library and the web to find other examples of murals to share with the class.

Introduce the students to the basic information about their mural by discussing the theme, site, time frame, and materials for the project.

Show them the size of the mural support—foam core, fabric, wood panels, or wall. Seeing is believing!

BRAINSTORMING

Within the chosen theme, the class will use brainstorming to arrive at the primary ideas for their mural.

Brainstorming is a process that involves gathering and expressing ideas, listing them, editing the list through discussion, and taking a series of votes to finalize the choices. This first step in collaboration insures a sense of ownership of the mural.

To select the mural themes, lead your class in this step-by-step brainstorming process.

- Compile a list on the board of all of the students' ideas relevant to the already chosen theme of the mural.

- When the list is complete, each student casts one vote for a favorite idea, reducing the list to four or five. Erase all the other ideas.

- This is followed by an often intense discussion that typically includes how to expand some ideas and make others more specific.

  - If the general subject is the undersea world, brainstorming may reveal a particular interest in shells, fish, and sunken treasure, or a desire to include a large variety of sea life.

  - Older students might choose a comparison of marine life in warm Caribbean waters and cold mountain lakes, or the myth of Neptune.

- Reviewing the results of these discussions, the major ideas emerge.

- To reach a consensus, a final vote is taken and the results are written down.

36. Fabric, high school (detail)

PICTURE FILE

Assemble a collection of pictures relevant to the subject of the mural to create a visual reference file.

The class will use this file to select particular images for the mural and the practice lessons.

- You probably have visual materials related to your mural subject in your classroom.

- Old issues of *National Geographic* are valuable resources for almost any subject.

- Tourist boards of most countries will gladly send promotional packets that contain excellent visual materials.

- Students can collect pictures from magazines, calendars, and web sites to add to the file.

IDENTIFYING SKILLS

Next, students identify the particular abilities they each bring to a mural-making collaboration. This form of self-assessment reassures students that they each have important abilities to contribute to the mural.

The list of skills goes well beyond drawing and painting.

- Using brainstorming, compile a list that should include imagination, cooperation, listening, taking turns, compromising, abstract thinking, concrete thinking, problem-solving, focusing, math skills, neatness. . . .
- Going through the list, ask students to identify each of their strengths.

An essential skill for all students is the ability to talk with civility to their classmates.

- Take turns expressing ideas.
- Disagree without being rude.
- **NEVER** insult anyone's art work.

COLLABORATION

Collaboration is the act of exchanging ideas, listening, compromising, and agreeing so that a group can successfully work for a common result.

Throughout the mural-making process, students are learning and practicing collaboration. It allows all students, on all skill levels, to fully participate and contribute to the big picture.

The teacher organizes the class into groups of at least three students with various skills who will work together throughout the project.

Return to the list of themes from brainstorming. The first collaborative job is to select which idea each group will work on to create a *piece* of the mural.

- In an undersea theme, one group might choose a sea horse, another a large fish or a school of small fish, a turtle, or coral, shells and plants.

Give each group images from the picture file that are appropriate to their themes. Groups discuss and informally choose the images that they like and feel comfortable drawing.

Choosing among the picture file images is not easy. Members of the group may like two or three different images. There are several strategies that can be helpful in making decisions.

- Combine the images.
- Go through the picture file for other options.
- Vote.

37. Picture file, 4th grade

After selecting and agreeing on images from the picture file, each group will ultimately create drawings based on those images.

Each group will need a folder in which to store their work-in-progress at the end of each session. Label the folder with a group number and the names of all the group members. Put the selected images into the folder.

THE SHAPE LESSON

Anyone approaching drawing may at first feel uncomfortable. The shape lesson has been developed to put both teachers and students at ease.

38. The shape lesson

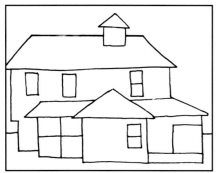

39. The shape lesson

40-41. The shape lesson

*42. Acrylic paint on plywood,
4th grade*

Every image can be simplified and understood as a combination of basic geometric shapes.

Taking turns at the board, several students draw and label the five basic shapes: circle, oval, rectangle, square, and triangle.

Select one simple and clear picture from the file as an example and hang it up.

- Point out each large shape and ask the class to identify it:
  - house / rectangle
  - flowers / circle
  - fish body / oval
- On the board, draw the shapes the class has identified in the same positions they occupy in the picture.
- When the shapes are assembled, they will recreate the basic image in the picture.
- Using other pictures, several students repeat this exercise on the board.
- Review with the class the three basic sequential steps of the shape lesson:
  - Find it.
  - Name it.
  - Draw it.

All students practice the shape lesson at their desks using any image from the picture file.

The shape lesson is the basis for all mural drawing. It will be mentioned often in other chapters.

Use it. It works!

This chapter has introduced the essential step-by-step common beginnings of all mural-making processes—choosing themes, brainstorming, creating a picture file, collaboration, and the shape lesson. It describes how a mural project can be a vehicle for integrating art with other curriculum and with educational objectives of collaboration. This kind of integrated, multilayered learning will continue throughout the creation of your mural.

If you are making a paper collage mural, go to Chapter Nine. For a fabric mural, go to Chapter Ten.

CHAPTER FOUR

THE PAINTED MURAL: MATERIALS AND TOOLS

THIS IS THE first of five chapters devoted to the painted mural. Here you will find practical and detailed information about the supports, paints, brushes, and other supplies necessary for making a painted mural, followed by a supply list and budget.

43. Painting materials and tools

There are two categories of supplies, materials and tools. Materials are consumable—supports, paints, varnishes; tools are reusable—brushes, drop cloths, scissors.

POSSIBLE PANEL ARRANGEMENTS

ONE PANEL
32 square feet

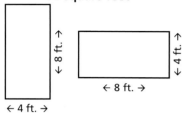

TWO PANELS
64 square feet

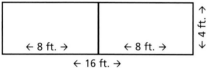

THREE PANELS
96 square feet

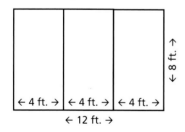

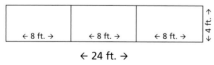

44. Options for arranging panels

SUPPORTS

The surface on which you paint your mural is technically called the support whether it is panels, a wall, or canvas to be affixed to a wall.

Panels are used for your support unless you are painting directly on the wall. We recommend that you select panels made of plywood or MDF (medium density fiberboard). These panels come in standard 4 x 8-foot sheets, ¼- or ½-inch thick. The ¼-inch panels are lightweight, easy to move, store, and install. However, they are not durable enough for exterior use. If you choose plywood, it must be a high quality grade with a smooth finish on at least one side. The *Tiffany* of plywoods is birch and, although it is more expensive, it does have a superior painting surface.

The number of panels you will need for your mural depends on the size of your space and your budget. It is certainly not necessary to cover the entire wall and you have many options for arranging the panels. In addition, when purchasing your

panels, the lumber yard can custom-cut a panel to fit the idiosyncrasies of a particular wall. In the example on the left, a 1 x 4-foot piece was custom-cut to fit the turn in the wall and continue the mural.

45. Acrylic paint on plywood, high school (detail)

The other option when choosing a support is to use an existing wall, interior or exterior, and paint directly on it. Walls or panels? As you make your choice, consider the following advantages and drawbacks of working directly on a wall.

ADVANTAGES

- Can create any size or unusual shape
- Can include doors as supports
- Saves the cost of wood
- No installation is needed
- No panels to set up and to store after each session
- Working upright, the mural is painted as it will be seen
- Other classes and teachers get to see the mural's process

DRAWBACKS

- Existing wall paint must be compatible with water-based latex primer.
- Students may have to stand on chairs or desks to reach the higher areas.
- Work is not done in a controlled classroom environment.
- Work can be disrupted by hallway traffic.
- For an interior wall with limited space, only half the class can work at one time. Where are the others, and with whom?
- Supplies must be carried to and from storage areas for each session.

If you choose to paint directly on the wall, measure and mark off the area you want to use. Calculate the number of square feet you will be painting.

Canvas is another option for a painted mural support. It can be used when a wall is in poor or fragile condition, or if the wall is made of a nonpaintable material like marble. Lightweight cotton canvas comes in many widths. It is bought by the yard and conveniently available already primed. Canvas murals can be installed using industrial velcro, grommets, or a sleeve and rod system.

WATER-BASED PRIMER

ALL mural supports must be primed, whether you are painting on panels, directly on a wall, or on canvas. Most house paint manufacturers make an all-purpose, interior/exterior latex primer that is suitable for all your mural surfaces. Be sure to specify **FLAT**, **WHITE**, **WATER-BASED LATEX**. **NEVER USE ANY OIL-BASED PRODUCTS**.

One gallon of primer should cover 250 square feet. Raw brick, cinderblock, or unpainted cement will absorb twice as much paint as nonporous surfaces.

WATER-BASED PAINTS

There are two main categories of paint—water-based (thinned with water) and oil-based (thinned with turpentine). Water-based paints are the only types appropriate for use in the classroom and the only ones we will discuss.

There are two options when choosing water-based paints for a mural—artist acrylics or water-based latex house paints. These types of paint share common advantages:

- They are available in a wide range of colors.
- They dry quickly.
- When dry, they are tough and water-resistant.
- Tools can be cleaned with soap and water.

ARTIST ACRYLICS

There are many brands of artist acrylics and, as with so many other products, you get what you pay for. We recommend Golden Artist Colors because they are easy to mix and to apply smoothly and evenly; they are heavy-bodied (less paint covers more surface); and they are durable and less likely to fade.

LATEX HOUSE PAINTS

Latex house paints lack some of the color intensity, body, and durability of artist acrylics, but they are much less expensive, making them an attractive alternative. We recommend Benjamin Moore paint because it offers an extensive range of colors, is uniform in quality, and is readily available.

We do not recommend mixing acrylics and house paints together. However, you *can* apply acrylics *over* house paint. You may, for economy, choose to cover large background areas with house paints and use artist acrylics for details.

HOW MUCH PAINT WILL YOU NEED?

The answer depends on the size of your support and the type and brand of paint you select. An ounce of Golden, because of its heavy body consistency, covers four times more surface than the same amount of house paint; nevertheless, house paints are always less expensive than artist acrylics.

ARTIST ACRYLICS

On a primed surface, interior or exterior, two quarts of artist acrylic should cover 100 square feet. We recommend a palette of ten colors and white that includes a range of primary and secondary colors (see budget on page 32 for details).

HOUSE PAINTS

The smallest can of latex house paint available is one quart. Therefore, regardless of the covering ratio, it is necessary to buy at least nine quarts of paint to have a basic range of colors – two quarts of white and one quart each of yellow, orange, red, purple, blue, green, and brown.

46. Acrylic paint on brick (detail)

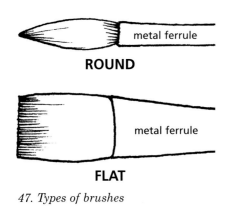

ROUND

FLAT

47. Types of brushes

BRUSHES

There is a seemingly infinite variety of brushes from which to choose, round and flat-shaped, made of bristle, hair, and synthetic materials. The nature and size of your support (panel or wall) and your paints help to narrow your selections.

- Synthetic (primarily nylon) brushes are made to stand up to the demands of artist acrylic paints.
- Bristle brushes are all-purpose, generally used with house paints and acrylics.
- Hair (sable, squirrel, camel) brushes are excellent for watercolors and oils but not for acrylics or house paints.

Synthetic and bristle brushes are appropriate for most of your mural needs. The size of the mural will affect your choice of brushes; the larger the mural, the more big brushes you will need. Synthetic ½-inch flat brushes will be used most often. Small synthetic round brushes are used for details. Rollers can be used for painting directly on very large walls.

DROP CLOTHS

The purpose of drop cloths is to keep the work site clean. There are two basic types—plastic and fabric. A roll of medium or heavy weight plastic should meet all your needs for covering desks and a supply table when using panels that are laying flat. For painting directly on a wall, use fabric drop cloths (or newspaper) for the floors. Plastic is too slippery.

Students should also wear smocks to protect their clothing. Some students prefer to change into their paint shirts while others like a big, roomy shirt to go over school clothes.

VARNISHES

Varnishing your mural protects the underlying surface and allows easy cleaning. Some varnishes offer additional protection by including ultraviolet light stabilizers to resist fading and discoloration. A coating of varnish is optional for interior murals and essential for exterior murals.

Here are some questions to consider before you purchase the supplies for your painted mural.

- What is your budget?
- How large will the mural be?
- Will it be interior or exterior?
- What supplies are already available?

BUDGET:
MATERIALS AND TOOLS FOR THE PAINTED MURAL

The cost of supplies for your painted mural depends primarily on the size you have selected. In all cases, it is important to use good quality materials and tools.

The prices listed here are based on one unit of an item. Prices may vary from location to location and year to year.

INTERIOR PAINTED MURAL

Plywood, sheet, 4-ft. x 8-ft., ¼- to ½-inch thick, finished on one side $25.00-50.00
MDF, sheet, 4-ft. x 8-ft., ¼- to ½-inch thick...$18.00-26.00
Primer, gallon, white, water-based, latex $17.00-20.00
Plastic drop cloth, roll, medium to heavyweight...$8.00
House paint brushes, 15, flat, assorted sizes, 1-in. to 2½-in............................$1.00-3.00
Artist paint brushes, 20, flat, ¼-in. to 1-in., small rounds...............................$3.00-7.00
House paint, quart, flat, water-based, latex $8.00-10.00
Two quarts white, 1 quart each yellow, orange, red, purple, blue, green, brown
Artist acrylic paints (prices vary widely according to color) – 4-ounce jar
(Two quarts – sixteen 4-ounce jars, covers about 100 square feet)

    titanium white (4 to 5 4-ounce jars)..$7.00
    primary yellow...$9.00
    diarylide yellow $14.00
    pyrrole or vat orange..$16.00
    napthol red medium $12.00
    medium magenta...$13.00
    permanent violet dark $14.00
    phthalo blue...$9.00
    ultramarine blue $8.00
    permanent green light $9.00
Newsprint paper pad, 14 x 17-in. or 17 x 24-in. $4.00-7.00
Brown kraft paper, roll, 2.5-ft. x 15-ft. $2.00
Saral transfer paper, package, red, blue or black...$12.00
Snap line with powder $10.00
Masking tape, 1-in. roll $1.00-2.00

Scissors, pencils, erasers, rulers, yardstick, buckets, paint shirts, bar soap,
liquid soap, paper towels, plastic water jars, cardboard, plastic mixing spoons

EXTERIOR PAINTED MURAL

Use the list above, with two exceptions. You must specify primer that is all-purpose or exterior.
An exterior mural should be sealed with a coat of compatible varnish on both sides of panels. A mural painted directly on the wall must also be sealed.
Exterior varnish, quart, water-based latex compatible $15.00-20.00
Mineral spirits, quart $4.00

CHAPTER FIVE

GIANT STEPS: PRIMING, DRAWING, AND COMPOSING

THIS CHAPTER ABOUT the painted mural addresses three essential steps in the process—priming, drawing, and composing.

PRIMING the panels is rather like whitewashing in the Mark Twain story of Tom Sawyer. Watching others and awaiting a turn is full of anticipation and excitement; the actual job of priming is concentrated physical work. Within the priming lessons, students are introduced to many of the skills and *housekeeping* routines that are fundamental to success in painting the mural.

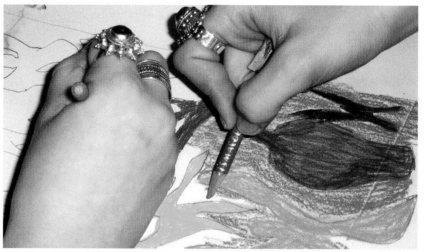

48. Drawing, high school

DRAWING is one of the foundations of mural-making. The drawings define the theme and are *parts* that will be assembled in composing to become the *whole*. In our mural process, drawing is a collaborative group activity, full of discussion, compromise, lines, and erasures.

COMPOSING, arranging all of the drawings into one coherent whole, is both intellectual and subjective. It calls on the class to act as a group, making choices, adding, rearranging, and editing. Composing is complex and challenging, involving decision-making based on the principles of art and intuition.

All of the pivotal steps in mural-making, priming, drawing, and composing, rely on different skills and approaches to individual work and collaboration. They each stretch different sets of both intellectual and physical muscles.

HOUSEKEEPING ROUTINE

The repetition of a routine helps students feel comfortable with their tools and materials and self-assured about what is expected of them.

The priming sessions, like all other painting sessions, begin with a consistent housekeeping routine, *setting up*.

- Put on paint shirts.
- Cover desks and supply table with drop cloths or newspaper.
- Organize the tools and materials on the supply table.
- Arrange the panels on the desks so that there is easy access to all sides of each one.

CARE OF BRUSHES

Lead a discussion about the appropriate uses and care of the brushes.

- Identify the different kinds of brushes and the parts of the brush. ☀ **CHAPTER FOUR – BRUSHES**
- Hold the brush between the ferrule, or metal part, and the wood, as you would hold a pencil.
- During each painting session, **ALWAYS** put brushes in water when they are not in use. Any paint left to dry in a brush will harden and make it useless.
- Carefully clean brushes with soap and water.
- Store clean brushes upright with the wooden ends down.

To get better aquainted with the sizes and properties of various brushes, each group takes a turn practicing on the board with different brushes, using water instead of paint.

49. Acrylic paint on plywood, high school (detail)

SUPPLIES

To cut down on trips to and from the sink, put two large buckets on the supply table, one full of clean water for filling water containers and one that is empty for dumping dirty water.

Creating a comfortable work environment has less to do with the size of the room than it does with the care of the supplies and the organization of the space.

An unimpeded path from the panels to the supply table creates a comfortable traffic flow.

At the beginning of each painting session, students will need a paint supply *setup kit*, assembled at the supply table.

- piece of heavy cardboard
- small plastic water container
- appropriate brush
- appropriate paint

CLEANING UP

Cleaning up is a crucial part of housekeeping. It should be routinized and done with the same care as setting up.

Each painting session ends with a basic cleaning-up routine.

- Wash brushes with soap and water and store them with tops up.
- Clean old paint out of the tops of the paint jars so they are easy to reopen.
- Add a small amount of water to any paints that seem too thick, and shake well.
- Store the paints upright, along with the brushes, in a milk crate or carton.
- If the panels are stacked for storage between painting sessions, cover each with clean plastic to protect the surface.
- Put away the color reference sketch carefully.

PRIMING

Priming the panels is necessary to seal the wood and to create an even white surface on which to draw and paint and also functions as a practice painting lesson.

At the supply table, shake the primer, pour it into wide-mouth containers to be shared by two or three students, and select large house paint brushes. Students assemble their paint *setup kits* and take them to the panels. Put all supplies on the pieces of cardboard, never directly on the panels. This helps students control their supplies and keeps the mural surface clean.

Priming must be done evenly in one direction. The primed panel should be smooth with no lumps, bumps, or streaks.

- Prime the finished or smoothest side of each panel.
- Prime the side edges carefully.
- Let the panels dry and apply a second coat.
- For exterior murals, prime both sides with two coats. Pay particular attention to the edges to insure a waterproof seal.

No more than six students can work on one panel when priming.

Students return to their group folders and practice drawing their selected images.

50. Priming, 4th grade

There are additional and significant jobs to be done while one or two groups are priming.

On large paper, several students make a list of the *setting up* and *cleaning up* housekeeping routines to be posted and referred to often.

With the priming completed, take time with the class to enjoy their accomplishments.

Lead a discussion of the talents and skills that will become most important as the mural process continues:
- stamina and patience
- drawing skills
- *advanced* collaborative skills
- attention to detail
- responsibility with materials

Drawing lays the groundwork for mural-making. Young children explore and develop ideas by drawing quickly and spontaneously. As older children develop new skills, they begin to represent subjects from observation, experience, and imagination.

Everyone wants to draw well. Some may be apprehensive at first. The shape lesson has been developed as both a learning activity and a practice lesson to put teachers and students at ease.

51. Drawing big, ages 11 to 15

Our process is based on drawing big. There is only one situation that uses small drawings. It involves a complex way to transfer the drawings called the grid method. This method is described in detail in Chapter Six.

DRAWING BIG

Student drawings will eventually be transferred to the panels or wall. Since murals are always large, the basic steps for drawing, and for transferring, are designed for big drawings.

Briefly review the shape lesson so that students will feel at ease as they begin to create their final drawings for the mural. ✷ **CHAPTER THREE – THE SHAPE LESSON**

Give each group pencils, erasers, and a sheet of drawing paper at least 17 x 24 inches on which to collectively draw their chosen image.

52. *Fabric, high school (detail)*

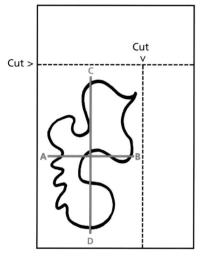

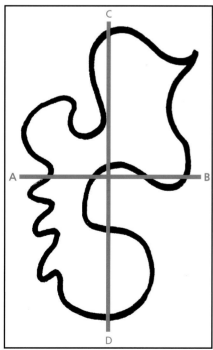

53. *Informal grid*

If the mural has one or two very large central images, combine several sheets of drawing paper to accommodate these *giant* drawings.

To facilitate large drawings, students should touch three lines to three edges of the paper. For example, when holding the paper vertically, a figure's head touches the top, feet touch the bottom, and one arm or hand touches a side edge of the paper.

If some students continue to make small drawings, hold their drawings up to the panel to see if they get lost on such a big support. Decide together how small is too small.

For students whose drawings are too small, encourage them to try again, touching the edges to emphasize *bigger*.

If students need further help in drawing **BIG**, demonstrate the informal grid or cross method of enlarging a drawing.

- Cut off the excess paper, leaving the small drawing on a rectangle or square.
- Draw an informal cross over the small drawing and label the cross lines A-B and C-D.
- On a much larger paper of the same shape, square or rectangle, draw a large informal cross.
- The cross creates four boxes on both the small and large papers. Each box will contain a small section of the total drawing.
- On the large paper, students draw the section of the image located in each box, one box at a time.
- The lines in each box of the small drawing must be drawn in the **SAME** box and position on the large paper.
- After the drawings have been enlarged, students can refine and add to the image.

Do not rush the drawing process. At the end of each drawing session, display all the work so the class can see what has been accomplished.

DETAILS

Details are an important addition to a work of art. They insure that images will be unique, specific, and engaging to look at.

54. Acrylic paint on plywood, 4th grade (detail)

Lay out all the drawings and ask the students to suggest what details can be added. The entire class should participate.

- Look for essential characteristic details and variety like the different sizes and shapes of windows and leaves, or stripes and spots on fish and cats.
- Avoid small generic details like fingernails.
- Encourage imagination and originality.

CLICHÉS

Even though students are using images from the picture file, they need some guidance on the subject of clichés.

A cliché in the visual arts is an image that has become overly familiar, trite, or commonplace. The inclusion of a cliché can make an otherwise excellent drawing boring or mundane.

- One of the most often used clichés is the *sun in the corner of the paper*. No one seems to know how this began. When it is pointed out, students immediately understand that, in fact, they have never seen a sun in the corner of the sky.
- Our list of clichés includes lollipop trees, hearts, rainbows, happy faces, hands clasped across the globe, half triangle noses, and squirrel holes in tree trunks.

Students should understand why they cannot use logos or other copywritten images such as Disney characters.

It is illegal to use logos and other copywritten materials without permission, even in a school mural. As an alternative, students can create their own logos, cartoon characters, or superheroes.

When the drawings are finished, students trim them with scissors, leaving about an inch of paper all around the image.

Lay these trimmed drawings out on the panels and ask the students:

- What images does the mural still need?
- Which images need further details?
- Which images need to be bigger or smaller?

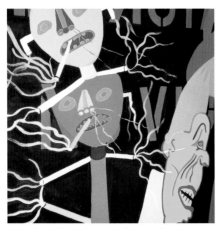

55. Acrylic paint on plywood, junior high school (detail)

It may turn out that no revisions or additions are needed, but if they are needed they should be made immediately so that the process can move along.

COMPOSING

Once the basic drawings have been completed, they must be organized into a unified arrangement. The pencil drawings are like small pieces of a large puzzle. As with a jigsaw puzzle, the appropriate placement of each piece is not, at first, always apparent.

In a work of art, the arrangement of parts to make a whole is called the composition. Composition has many functions.

- It provides a sense of unity so that the artwork is complete.

- It creates a harmonious effect with nothing out of place.

- It presents the theme clearly.

- It directs the viewer's eye to move around the work.

In a work of art, the arrangement of parts to make a whole is called the composition. Composition has many functions.

- It provides a sense of unity so that the artwork is complete.

- It creates a harmonious effect with nothing out of place.

- It presents the theme clearly.

- It directs the viewer's eye to move around the work.

When composing, take lots of time and take liberties.

☀ CHAPTER TWO – APPROACHES TO COMPOSING A MURAL

- Pieces of the puzzle will be moved around many times. Rearranging or moving one or two drawings when composing will affect the others.

- There is a great deal of intuition and trial and error involved in composing. Your eyes will instinctively recognize the inept and awkward, the graceful, the original, and the powerful.

- Unusual placements may defy logic, but can add surprise, humor, emphasis, and balance. For example, a boat might sail in the sky; a group of images could be stacked like a totem pole.

- A cutout of a drawing can be used as a template (to draw around). Try repeating the image in a variety of positions or using it to create a larger area of interest by grouping the repeated image.

56. Acrylic paint on plywood, 3rd / 4th grades (detail)

How will you know when the composition is *right*? Beyond trusting your eyes and intuition, use the example of how to apply the **PRINCIPLES** at the end of Chapter Two as a guide.

FINALIZING THE COMPOSITION

To continue involving the principal in the mural process, show him/her the completed drawing composition for feedback.

There are three remaining steps to complete the composing process.

If you have composed on panels:

- A group of students make a rough drawing of the images and their placements in relation to one another. This sketch will be duplicated for each group and used later for a color plan.

- With a pencil, lightly mark the placement of each drawing on the panels.

- Remove the drawings from the panels and carefully store them.

- On masking tape, label each of these areas with the group name.

With the priming, drawing, and composing complete, your panels have been transformed. Where last week you had empty wood, you now have a clean white surface with all the drawings positioned, marked, and ready to be transferred. The students have gained and used an impressive range of new skills. Pause, applaud, and prepare to plunge ahead.

57. Primed site

CHAPTER SIX

LOW TECH/HIGH TECH: TRANSFERRING AND ENLARGING

IN OUR CURRENT high-tech world, the techniques discussed here for transferring and enlarging mural drawings could be viewed as antiquated. Old-fashioned as the following four methods—outlining, using transfer paper, creating *carbon paper*, and the traditional grid method—may seem, they are, in fact, entirely appropriate and efficient.

58. Using transfer paper, 4th grade

What is transferring? Transferring is a method of moving the drawings from one surface (paper) to another more permanent surface (the support). When transferring, students, who up to this point have been doing individual group work, will now see all of their drawings become the mural's composition.

Taking small group images and transforming them into giant mural narratives is always exciting.

DIRECT TRANSFER METHODS
OUTLINING

We begin by presenting three direct transfer methods using large drawings. The outlining method is fast, easily comprehensible, immediately gratifying, and tidy.

59. Outlining, 4th grade

Take out the stored completed drawings. Student monitors distribute the drawings.

- Students precisely cut out their drawings following along the outside edges. Do not cut out the lines.
- Take each cut drawing to the panels.
- Find the area marked on the panels for the drawings. Tape the drawings to the panel.
- Groups carefully outline their drawing in pencil.
- Remove the drawings and use for reference.
- Students *replicate* the details of the drawings on the panels using a freehand drawing style.
- Store the drawings. Panels are ready to be painted.

TRANSFER PAPER DEMONSTRATION

Using transfer paper is similar to using *old-fashioned* carbon paper. It can easily be used collaboratively and aids in precision work. The results are reliable and satisfying.

Use a small sample to show how the transfer paper works.

- Make a paper *sandwich*—white paper on the bottom, transfer paper with coated side down in the middle, and drawing on the top.
- Slowly draw over the lines pressing firmly with a pen.
- Lift the transfer paper and drawing. Surprise!

USING TRANSFER PAPER

We use Saral brand transfer paper which is expensive but can be reused many times.

If you use Saral transfer paper, choose a color that will show up on the primed panel, such as red or blue.

- Roll out Saral with coated side down.
- Place drawings on top of Saral.
- Tape drawings to Saral with small pieces of masking tape since the transfer paper is delicate.
- Cut the Saral to separate one drawing from another.

With the coated side down, following the design sketch, tape the transfer paper and drawings to the primed panels.

Students trace their drawings with a colored pen. The color helps them to see where they have traced.

- When the tracing is complete, remove the tape, separate the drawings from the transfer paper, and set both aside.
- The panels are ready to be painted.

60. Using transfer paper, 5th / 6th grade

CREATING CARBON PAPER

Creating *carbon paper* is an appropriate method of transferring drawings if Saral is not available or included in your budget. While this process is not time-consuming nor expensive, it can be messy.

Students cut out their drawings (similar to the **OUTLINING** method).

Students hold drawings up to a window or light box with the **BACK** of the drawing facing them.

- Take a pencil and cover the interior lines of the drawing that show through. We recommend using a 3B or Ebony pencil. Press hard to completely cover the lines.
- Place and tape the drawings face up on the primed panels in the same position as the design sketch.
- Carefully outline the drawings with a pencil.
- Students trace over the interior lines by pressing hard with a colored pen. This process will leave a pencil line on the panels.
- When this transfer process is complete, carefully remove the *carbon paper* drawings and set them aside.

Students are always surprised and full of pride when they see the results. The panels are ready to be painted.

TRADITIONAL GRID METHOD FOR ENLARGING

Enlarging drawings requires hard work and concentration. The traditional grid method is a way to enlarge drawings and at the same time transfer them to the panels. It is more complex and challenging than the transfer methods previously mentioned.

The grid method requires patience, accuracy, time, and focus. Students who have taken on this challenge and learned it have come out with an enormous sense of mastery.

The traditional grid method for enlarging is recommended for grades 4 and up.

Introduce this method by defining a grid.

- It can be explained as a series of squares similar to graph paper.
- See Figure A on the following page.
- Measure each panel exactly.

CREATING A TRACING PAPER GRID

There are four separate steps to the grid method:

1. Creating a small tracing paper grid.

2. Creating a large scale primed panel/wall grid.

3. Composing the mural images on the small tracing paper grid.

4. Transferring the composition to the primed panels/wall.

At the conclusion of the last step, the mural drawing is ready to be painted.

To create a small manageable-sized grid on which to compose your mural, choose an appropriate scale with which to work. One foot (on the panel) = 2 inches (on the tracing paper), or 1 foot = 3 inches, or 1 foot = 4 inches scale.

- If your mural panels are 4 x 16 feet (Figure A), we suggest a 1 foot = 3 inches scale so that your drawing will be large enough to see clearly but not so large as to be difficult to handle. (12 x 48 inches)

- Draw this small grid on a piece of tracing paper. Measure carefully. Use a ruler to be precise.

- Use a colored pen for the grid lines to distinguish them from the pencil drawings to be added later.

- Number the vertical lines, left to right, at the top and bottom of the grid.

- Letter the horizontal lines, top to bottom, at both ends and in the middle if there are two combined panels. (See Figure A)

FIGURE A
Two Panels Together – 4 feet x 16 feet

61. The tracing paper grid

PRACTICE SNAP LINE TECHNIQUE

Just as the tracing paper grid needs accurate, straight lines, the large scale grid also requires accurate and straight lines.

A snap line, our version of high tech equipment, is a primary tool for putting a grid on any support. It is the easiest tool for making a straight line between two points.

Students learn to use the snap line by practicing on the board.

- Place two dots on the board at least two feet apart.

- Student A holds the snap line flat in his/her hand with the moveable part facing up.

- Student B pulls out the chalked string, places the metal end on one of the dots under his thumb, pressing down.

- Student A puts her end of the chalked string on the other dot, making sure that the string is tight.

62. Snap line

- Student C gently pulls the chalked string out (not more than two inches) and lets it snap against the board, leaving a straight chalk line.

- This is done both vertically and horizontally.

- After each use, the string is rewound and the snap line is shaken so that the string is rechalked.

PRIMED PANEL/WALL GRID

Measure and mark every 12 inches along all four sides of each panel. (See Figure A)

- Connect the marks with the snap line.

- First snap the vertical (shorter lines), and then the horizontal lines.

- With a ruler, remeasure one or two 12-inch squares for accuracy.

- Using the same numbers and letters from the tracing paper grid, label the lines on the panels.

The grid is a device for moving from small images to large. You already have the small tracing paper grid, and must now make the corresponding large grid on the panels or wall.

COMPOSING ON THE TRACING PAPER GRID

You are now ready to arrange your drawings into a final composition that will be traced onto the small paper grid. Trim the excess paper around the drawings to see their sizes more clearly. Follow the process: ⋅👁⋅ **CHAPTER FIVE – COMPOSING**

- Lay out the tracing paper grid.

- Arrange the drawings on top of the grid to see how they relate to the scale.

- When all the images are in place, use a pencil to lightly mark their positions.

- On the **BACK** of the tracing paper grid, tape the drawings into place as marked.

- Carefully trace the drawings onto the grid with a sharp pencil or pen.

- Remove the taped drawings and store them.

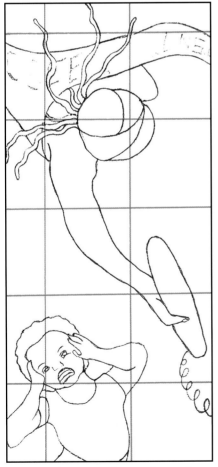

63. Drawings traced onto the tracing paper grid

FIGURE B

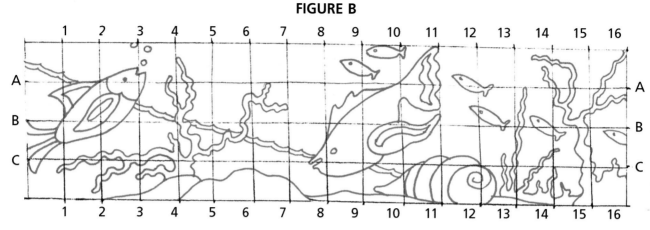

64. Small scale drawing on the tracing paper grid

Consider the design on the tracing paper a map of the mural. Now see if your students can read the map and find their way on the panels/wall.

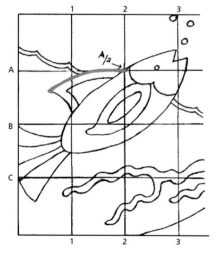

65. Enlargement on the panel of a section of Figure B

PRACTICING TRANSFERRING

Figure B is an example of how to begin transferring, using the grid method.

- Find the top of the fin of the fish (begins at A/2).
- On the panel, find A/2. Have a student mark it with a light chalk dot.
- Locate where the fin ends (left of line 1 and between A and B). Put a chalk dot at that spot.
- Connect the two dots to create the proper place for the top shape of the fin.

Each group practices transferring on the panels using a copy of their tracing paper drawing.

TRANSFERRING THE DRAWINGS

Working in groups, using chalk, the class transfers the entire composition to the primed panels/wall. After this step is completed, students

- redraw the chalk lines with pencil.
- remove the chalk lines and grid lines with a damp sponge.

The panels are ready for painting.

Having composed, transferred, and drawn their design on the primed panels/wall, students have completed about 40% of the process and about 70% of the *head work*.

CHAPTER SEVEN

RED CAT/PURPLE TREES: COLOR AND TECHNIQUE

YOUR STUDENTS ARE eager to paint. "Are we painting today? Please, please, can we paint now?" The two remaining steps before your students paint are choosing and mixing colors. Selecting colors calls upon the students to use skills they have already developed – working within their groups, brainstorming, and reaching consensus as a class. The process of mixing colors will be your time alone to explore, experiment, and experience a unique part of mural-making. When the colors have been mixed, the class can move on to a practice painting lesson.

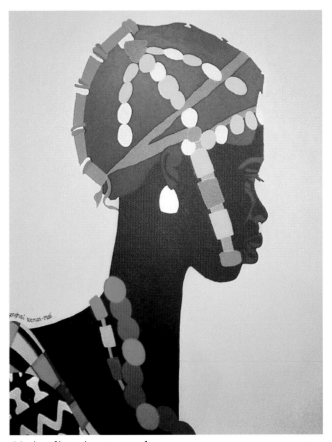

66. Acrylic paint on panel,
Shicoff and Braun-Reinitz (detail)

Color is transformative, carries meaning and associations and, like a magnet, draws you into the painting and powerfully holds you.

67. Acrylic paint on brick, high school (detail)

SELECTING COLORS

Each group gets a copy of the mural composition on which they will invent a color system.

- Display one copy of the mural composition for a class discussion of color possibilities.

- Without guidance you may find that students choose very representational colors.

- For your mural to be visually interesting and engaging, students need to be more imaginative and less traditional in their use of color.

☀ CHAPTER TWO – COLOR

Begin by asking about unusual ways to think about color. Choice of colors is very intuitive. **TRUST YOUR EYES**.

- Discuss the possible location, time of day, or season of your class composition. For example, in Figure A, the location could be the Caribbean, ocean, or fish tank.

- If people are part of your mural, skin color should be part of the conversation.

    - In our experience, the best option is to abandon representational skin colors in favor of variations of orange, purple, green, and blue.

    - Since these colors are not real skin colors, they can represent all people rather than specific races.

    - Show examples of pictures or postcards of paintings where skin color is used in innovative or eccentric ways.

- You can apply nonrepresentational color to everything in your mural.

    - For example, the sky need not be blue nor tree trunks brown.

    - Think about a red Statue of Liberty, yellow bridges, lavender wolves, orange houses, a blue pyramid.

Students collaborate on creating their group color system.

- Using markers, students color their copy of the mural composition.

- Do not use black or brown markers.

The class will produce one final color guide arrived at by consensus. Display all the finished group copies.

68. Acrylic paint on brick, ages 12 to 14

- It is easy to start talking about color choices by looking at the largest area of color, since this color will dominate. ·☼· **CHAPTER TWO – EMPHASIS**

- All other colors relate to the largest area. For example, the biggest shape in Figure A is the top of the water. The next shape you might consider is one that is central in placement or importance to the narrative.

FIGURE A

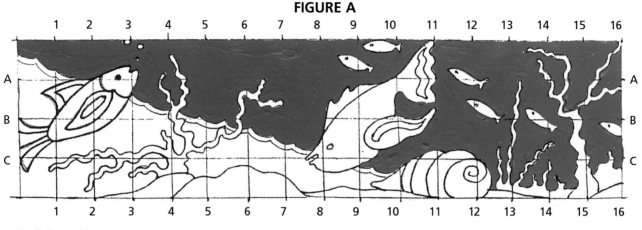

69. Color guide

To continue brainstorming about the groups' color choices, consider:

- What colors are repeated to get your eye to move across the picture?

- What color combinations catch your eye? Why?

- If the water surrounding the body of the **BIG** fish in Figure A is blue/purple, the fish could be a complementary color such as orange or hot pink.

Why would you encourage your students to pick unexpected colors?

- To avoid stereotypes

- To create drama and surprise

- To open up more options for the other colors

Students make the final color decisions for each area by consensus beginning with the largest area.

On one clean sketch, have several students fill in the final color choices using markers.

PAINT MIXING FOR TEACHERS

In spite of our emphasis on the benefits of collaboration, it is our experience that it is easier and more efficient if the colors are mixed without student participation. It can be done, but teaching students how to mix paint adds at least 5 or 6 class hours to the project. It is also difficult to supervise the mixing of paint with a large group. However, you may choose to demonstrate for the class how one or two colors are mixed.

When mixing paint, it is important for you to be physically comfortable.
⸰̇☀̇⸰ CHAPTER FIVE – HOUSEKEEPING ROUTINE

An orderly and clean space should be devoted to paint mixing.

You are now ready to embark on the adventure of paint mixing. Looking at all the paints spread out before you, how do you estimate the amount of paint to mix for each shape?

There is no precise formula, but with some practice you will become more confident and develop better *guesstimation* skills.

- In Figure A (page 49), the biggest shape is the top water which runs through the mural on a diagonal. It is probably more than half of the total surface.
- You will also notice that the **BIG** fish, shell, and other objects take up a considerable amount of space. For this top water shape, you will be safe if you mix about 32 ounces of paint.

SAMPLE COLOR MIXING

In mixing paint, you will have the opportunity to create a family of reds, blues, greens, yellows, purples, and oranges in an array of subtle colors which include their tints and shades.

In order to arrive at a satisfying range of colors, you will need to experiment with color mixing in small quantities.

- Use the color guide as reference.
- Mix the biggest shape first.
- Always put the lightest color into the mixing container first. Add darker colors a little at a time.
- You may choose to use some colors directly from the jar.
- Brush a small sample on a piece of white paper to see the *real* color. Acrylic paint dries slightly darker.
- Place your dried samples next to each other to see the color combinations and contrasts.

MIXING IN QUANTITY

When you have all the sample colors, mix the appropriate quantity of each.

It is always wise to mix more paint than you think you will need and have leftovers rather than the alternative of mixing too little and running out.

70. Acrylic paint on brick and cinder block, ages 11 to 15

Keeping track of all the colors is very easy if some basic organizational methods are followed.

- To insure that the paint is thoroughly mixed, use a plastic mixing container that is considerably bigger than the amount of paint you are mixing.
- Pour the paint into several small jars so that a particular color can be used by students working at different places on the mural.

All paint jars need to be labeled.

- Put a piece of masking tape on the side of the jar.
- With a dark marker, write the name of the color (for example, **TOP WATER BLUE**)
- On the **TOP** of the jar lid, mark a dot of paint so you will know what color is inside.
- Write the name of each color on the final color design to identify the right color for the appropriate place.

PRACTICE PAINTING LESSON

⋅☼⋅ CHAPTER FIVE — HOUSEKEEPING ROUTINE

The first encounter with painting has finally arrived. The practice painting lesson is a time of concentration and focus.

Distribute one piece of white paper, a pencil, a small brush, and cardboard to each student. Give each table a small amount of paint (use one color) and a container of water. Students draw several large geometric shapes freehand on white paper.

Demonstrate how to paint.

- Hold the brush as you would a pencil, relaxed, above the ferrule or metal part of the brush.
- Wet the brush. Squeeze out extra water.
- Dip the brush into the paint only on the bristles, not covering the metal.
- Brush excess paint off on the side of the jar.
- Paint the shape by brushing on the paint in one direction up to the lines.
  - There should be no white paper showing inside the shape.
  - Put the brush into the water when not in use. (Acrylic paint will harden and cannot be removed from the brush.)

71. Practice painting lesson, 4th grade

Remind students that this painting procedure is similar to the way in which they primed their panels/wall. But here they use only a small brush and small amount of paint.

Cleanup. ⋅☼⋅ **CHAPTER FIVE – HOUSEKEEPING ROUTINE**

Through this practice lesson, students acquire new skills which can be reviewed.

What have you learned in this practice painting lesson?

- How to hold and control a small brush.
- How much paint to put on a small brush.
- How to paint inside a shape.
- How to care for the brushes.

Students everywhere delight in and are awed by working with color. You, the teacher, have done an enormous amount of time-consuming work to prepare your class for their exciting painting experience. Mixing beautiful colors and applying them is challenging and complex. As students become more sensitive to color relationships and nuances, they are able to understand and use the family of colors freely and imaginatively. They will carry this knowledge with them always.

72. Acrylic paint on plaster, high school (detail)

CHAPTER EIGHT

FROM PAINTING TO APPLAUSE: PAINTING, REFINING, INSTALLING, AND CELEBRATING

"PLEASE, PLEASE, ARE we painting **TODAY**?" The answer is emphatically **YES**. In the next eight to ten sessions your class will paint and paint, refine, edge, and paint some more until the mural is finished.

73. Refining

Now the process goes back to the two people with whom you consulted in the original proposing stage. The custodian is needed for installing the mural and the principal is asked to participate in the official celebration when the entire school community can come together to applaud your class achievement.

HOUSEKEEPING

With your mural composition drawn on the panels/wall, your newly acquired knowledge about painting, and a color map, the students are well-prepared to begin painting their mural.

Review. **CHAPTER FIVE — HOUSEKEEPING ROUTINE**

- Place the panels on a flat surface.
- On the supply table, lay out only the paints and brushes you will be using for the large shapes.
- Group the paints according to their color family.
- Help the students assemble their paint setup kits.
- Have the groups take their setup kits to the location of their images on the panels.

74. Respecting the drawing, high school (detail)

RESPECTING THE DRAWING

The students have put an enormous amount of effort into the quality of their drawings and the composition. Without painting experience, they do not have the skill to paint close to the lines of their images.

It is essential that students be able to see and keep track of the images until the refining step. Therefore, students **DO NOT** paint up to the drawing outlines or over the lines.

- Leave ½ to 1 inch around each shape.
- Students need to **SEE** what this means.
- Demonstrate with a large brush on a panel.

PAINTING LARGE SHAPES

Students learn to paint their mural by *doing*. The easiest and most efficient way for them to gain experience is to paint the large shapes first.

While painting the large shapes, students:

- Use large brushes for large shapes.
- Hold and control their brush properly.
- Know how much paint to put on the brush.
- Paint smoothly and evenly in the same direction.
- Paint carefully and slowly.
- **DO NOT** paint up to the image outline.

At the end of each large shape painting session, put the panels together and look at what has been done.

- How do the shapes look now that they are **BIG**?
- How effectively are the colors working together?
    - If a shape looks too bright, or dark or dull, it can be changed.
    - For example, if a red is too bright, don't abandon red. Soften it by adding a small amount of a complementary color. ⋅👁⋅ **CHAPTER TWO — COLOR**

PAINTING MID- AND SMALL-SIZE SHAPES

As students move on to painting mid- and small-size shapes, you can see them gaining more proficiency, confidence, and independence.

While the painting process is always basically the same, some practical adjustments are made when working with smaller shapes.

- Smaller brushes are used.
- The pace slows down.
- Be prepared for a certain amount of student frustration since it looks as though less work is being done.

ASSESSING PROGRESS

During most of the painting process, your mural will look incomplete, messy, and disconnected. It is appropriate for the mural to look this way and it is not unusual to wonder if the mural will ever look coherent.

It is very helpful to talk about this unfinished look with your students. The most obvious reason for this incomplete appearance is the existence of the one-inch spaces around the shapes. The first step for *pulling the mural together* is to fill those spaces.

75. Refining, high school (detail)

COMPLETING THE SPACES

Students carefully paint the ground color up to edge line of the shape.

- Use ½-inch brush for this job.
- Working with the interior shape color, paint **ONTO** the shape outline.

What's next?

- Give the **BIG** areas a final even coat of paint where needed and touch up little drips or dirty areas.

REFINING

Refining — outlining and edging — creates a consistent, neat look. As the work becomes more precise, the number of students who are actually painting decreases.

This fact raises two questions:

- How are the eight to ten final painters chosen?
    - Within each group, students decide who can best do this work.
    - Or from your observation, select those students who can best do these jobs.
- What is the rest of the class doing?
    - The remaining students write about the mural project — the theme, the process, and skills learned. This writing will become part of the celebration.

Throughout the mural process, all the students have collaborated equally in all the steps. But now, in the refining phase, not all students have the skills necessary to participate in this type of work.

OUTLINING

In order to be effective, outlines need to be wide enough to be seen from a distance (¼ inch). Students choose what shapes need to be outlined.

- Outlines help to
    - emphasize the narrative
    - bring a lost image into view
    - focus on the negative shapes
    - correct messy edges
- Avoid using black. Instead, select complementary colors that work well with the ground and shape colors.

   **CHAPTER TWO — COLOR**

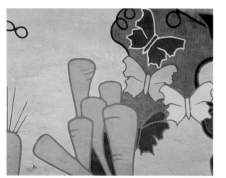

76. Outlining, ages 10 to 13 (detail)

If your mural contains BIG, simple shapes and you want to add extra visual interest or clarity, outlining the shapes is a perfect solution.

EDGING

Edging is time-consuming and requires a meticulous effort. When done properly, it clearly reinforces the integrity of each shape and of the composition.

- Always use the darker color of the figure-ground relationship for edging.
- Use your smallest brush.
- Anchor your hand on the panel.
- Paint in a continuous downstroke line.
- The students selected for outlining and edging practice on paper to find the flat brush that best suits them.

77. Edging, high school (detail)

78. Completion, ages 14 to 17 (detail)

The painting of your mural is COMPLETE! Sometimes the process has been tedious, sometimes arduous, often gratifying, and obviously productive.

Before the installation you have to consider whether or not to varnish the mural. Varnish is a clear liquid protective coating that is OPTIONAL for interior murals but NECESSARY for the longevity of exterior murals.

Only teachers and older students should work with this material.

WHEN TO STOP PAINTING

Somewhere between rushing to get through the painting and endlessly refining, the mural itself will tell you when to stop working. ·҉· **CHAPTER TWO – UNITY**

TITLE AND SIGNAGE

Titling your mural is an important part of the mural-making process.

- Students enjoy the collective task of choosing a title.
- Students brainstorm ideas for a title.
- A colon can be used both for description and variation. For example, *Sacred Sites: Myths and Legends*.
- Decide on one title by consensus.

Students' names and class are placed near the title.

- Signage can be created by hand or computer-generated.
- This signage can be inexpensively framed and hung near the mural.

VARNISHING EXTERIOR PANELS

To get the feel of the varnishing process, do the back first, painted side second, and the edges last.

- In a well ventilated area, lay the panels down flat.
- See the supply list for the suggested varnish.
    - Dilute only in glass containers
    - **NEVER** use shellac.
- Use a new 2-inch synthetic brush.
- Work quickly in one direction.
- Do not go over areas you have already done.
- Avoid puddles.
- With a smaller brush, carefully varnish the edges to seal them completely.

VARNISHING AN EXTERIOR WALL

The varnishing process is basically the same for walls as for panels. It is equally important to varnish in one direction.

Because the wall is vertical, pay particular attention to the possibility of drips.

INSTALLATION

If you have completed a panel mural, it must now be installed.

Meet with your custodian, review the site, and set a date for the installation. Be sure that you leave enough time to plan your celebration.

PLANNING THE CELEBRATION

You have done it all—from choosing a subject to planning the installation of your finished mural with the custodian. It is time to prepare for the celebration and reflect on the accomplishments of your class. Additional educational activities would be for students to assess the entire process and write or speak in public.

Before the celebration, have all the students write about the mural project—the theme, the art process, collaboration, and the skills they have gained.

- Selections from the writing can be posted next to the mural, in the hall near your room, or put together into a booklet distributed at the celebration.

The basic celebration generally includes:

- Taking photographs of the students with the mural
- Giving out a certificate of achievement to each student
- Asking the principal to speak and hand out certificates
- Inviting other classes, staff, and parents
- Having students create the invitation and program and speak about the mural process

To add further excitement for everyone, cover the mural with paper or a sheet until the celebration and reveal the finished mural to lots of applause and smiles.

After the spotlight of the celebration has dimmed, it is not unusual to experience a collective letdown, but remember that on a daily basis you and your class will be encountering your **BIG** achievement. Your mural is a permanent gift to the school community and will be seen and appreciated by future generations of students, staff, and families.

79. Acrylic paint on plywood, 5th/6th grades

CHAPTER NINE

PAPER MAGIC: THE COLLAGE MURAL

A COLLAGE IS made by arranging and pasting torn or cut pieces of paper on a support surface to create a visual statement. Collage was *invented* in the early twentieth century; today it has a permanent place among two-dimensional art media along with painting, drawing, and printmaking.

80. Paper on foam core, 2nd grade (detail)

The paper mural is particularly appropriate for young children, kindergarten through second grade. The materials are easy to work with and the process is full of opportunities for experimentation. The mural can be completed in about ten hours divided into sessions that suit the attention span of your class.

81. Torn paper, 6th grade

MATERIALS AND TOOLS

There are two categories of supplies—materials (consumable) such as paper and glue sticks, and tools (reusable) such as scissors and rulers. It is wise to assemble all of your supplies before you begin the project.

The support is the surface on which the mural is made. For a collage mural, your support will be foam core or heavy paper.

- We recommend 20 x 30-inch sheets of ¼-inch thick foam core which comes in white and assorted colors. Three or four sheets can be arranged in a variety of configurations, using up to four colors. In addition, foam core sheets are lightweight but sturdy and easy to store.

- The color of your support will influence the other color choices made throughout the making of the mural. When using foam core, you can combine colors.

  - Use the three primary colors.

  - Alternate complementary colors.

  - Use two sheets of a lighter color bounded by two of a darker color.

  - Avoid the lightest colors that get dirty easily.

- Your theme may suggest a color choice. For example, in a rainforest mural with many green elements, a green background would be the least suitable color choice.

- Climate, seasons, and time of day or night may suggest a background color or colors.

- Your second choice for a support is a roll of very heavy colored or white paper, at least 24 inches in height. It is less expensive than foam core. To enhance its durability, add a line of masking tape around the edges on the back.

- Do not use cardboard.

We recommend Fiskar scissors that can be used by both left and right handers. They are well-engineered and durable.

Small glue sticks of any brand are the best choice for an adhesive. Do not use a white glue like Elmer's that wrinkles the paper and is often messy.

A variety of colored and patterned papers can be used to create the collage elements. You will find a list of papers as well as a budget for supplies at the end of this chapter.

DEFINING A MURAL

It is important for you to review and become comfortable with "Five Easy Pieces"

·ᐧᐧ CHAPTER 3

The ideas, techniques, and sequences presented there will be directly applied to creating your paper mural.

Explain to the class what a mural is. With your students, make a list on the board of the properties that define it:

- large scale
- site specific
- narrative/tells a story
- seen by a large audience

To help students explore the topic of murals further, see the sequence of questions in Chapter Three.

DEFINING A COLLAGE

The examples you have discussed are probably big, painted murals. How can paper collage be used to create a mural? Make a simple collage with one big image and two or three details to use as an example.

Explain what a collage is and show the class your sample. With your students, list the properties that define it:

- pieces of cut or torn paper
- arranged to create visual images
- glued to a paper support
- the smallest details are made of paper
- nothing is drawn

By seeing the size and scale of the support, students readily understand the commitment and the time that will be needed to create their mural.

Show students the selected support. Discuss the schedule for making the mural. Students respond positively to a regular schedule. To hold their interest and enthusiasm, schedule mural classes at least twice a week, more often if possible.

COLLABORATION

You, as the teacher, will choose how to organize the next steps according to your personal management style.

Follow the steps in Chapter Three – Collaboration. Divide the class into working groups of three or more students. Each group sits together around one large work surface.

- Have students identify the skills they will bring to the collaboration.
- Use brainstorming techniques to select the mural ideas.
- Assemble a collection of images to create a picture file.
- Set up consistent housekeeping routines.

A comfortable arrangement of your room and the appropriate packaging and distribution of tools and materials for each hands-on session will help to insure a calm and focused classroom.

Each group will need one folder that is closed on three sides for storing their work in progress. Each folder should be labeled with the names of all the group members. Groups can make their own folders as a first group project.

At the end of each hands-on session, store finished images, works-in-progress, and paper scraps in the group folders.

THE COLLAGE SHAPE LESSON

The shape lesson in Chapter Three really works! Although the paper mural will not involve drawing, the shape lesson is essential to helping students understand all of their images in terms of shape.

Lead your students through the shape lesson beginning with "every picture can be simplified and understood as a combination of basic geometric shapes."

PRACTICE CUTTING AND GLUING LESSON

It has been our experience that, while most students have been taught scissor *etiquette*, how to hold and pass scissors, they have not been taught how to cut with them.

Demonstrate how to cut properly.

- Cut with the paper on the desk. Do not hold it in the air.
- Cut away from your body.
- Cut in from the edges of the paper.
- To change directions, stop, remove the scissors, reposition the paper, and cut again.
- Turn the paper rather than your hands and scissors.

The old adage that practice makes perfect is as applicable and as important to the visual arts process as it is to reading, math, music, and sports. It gives each student the opportunity to improve skills and gain confidence.

Demonstrate how to use glue sticks properly.

- Only a small amount of glue stick should be rolled out.
- Do not press hard on the stick.
- Always close the cover to avoid the glue drying out.

DIRECT CUTTING

Direct cutting means exactly what it says—cutting shapes from paper without drawing them first. This idea, that can be explained as drawing with scissors, reinforces the technique of creating with shapes. Even the smallest detail is a cut shape – a button (circle), window (rectangle), bird's beak (triangle).

Demonstrate for your students this lesson that combines the shape lesson, direct cutting, and the use of the glue sticks.

- Using a picture file image, identify and name the largest shape in the picture.
- Without drawing, cut a similar shape from a piece of practice paper.
- Identify two or three smaller shapes in the picture to cut out of practice paper.
- For this lesson, do not choose interior details.

82-83. Direct cutting of shapes using the picture file

Cover the desks with newspaper or drop cloths. Distribute an image from the picture file, practice paper, glue stick, and scissors to each student. Students practice direct cutting.

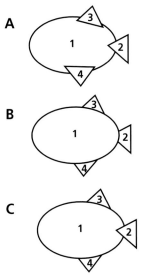

84. Assembling and gluing geometric shapes

Take time at this important juncture to discuss the skills students have learned by practicing cutting and gluing.

ASSEMBLING AND GLUING

The four cut geometric shapes can now be assembled to reconstruct the image from the picture file. There are several options for combining/overlapping as seen on the left.

- All three small shapes can be glued on top of the big shape. (A)
- All three small shapes can be glued in back of the big shape. (B)
- One small shape can be glued on top and two in back. (C)

Students should experiment with the combinations.

To assemble the pieces, carefully put a small amount of glue on the edges of the paper. Neatness counts! Additional glue for reinforcement can be added later as needed.

Ask your students which of their skills have improved. What have they learned by practicing that they did not know before?

CHOOSING GROUP IMAGES

Return to the list of themes and ideas the class has selected to include in their mural.

- Each group chooses one of the ideas to work on.
- Students use the picture file to find the specific images they will need to express their ideas.
- After studying the pictures, they can proceed in several ways:
    - Use one picture.
    - Combine parts of several pictures.
    - Create purely imaginary elements.
    - Combine real and imaginary elements.

85. Emphasis-varying sizes, 2nd grade (detail)

Sizes of images can vary for emphasis. In the example at the left, one group made an enormous figure stretching from the top to the bottom of the support. Another group made a series of trucks and cars, one of which is seen on the left.

CREATING THE GROUP IMAGES

Using the techniques from the direct cutting practice lesson, groups begin to create their images.

PAPERS

Your students will be seeing a vast array of papers for the first time, matte, shiny, rough, and patterned. It is fun to get acquainted with this medium.

86. Combining papers, 6th grade

Distribute collage papers for each group in shallow containers—baskets, shoe boxes, pie tins. Each group's container should include a selection of the basic colors and kinds of papers, plus some unique patterned papers.

Encourage students to try combinations of papers that will add visual interest to the collage.

- The assortment of papers can be used in unorthodox ways. A tree trunk can be red or patterned, a building striped, a person purple with orange arms.
- Save some special papers to introduce later in the process.
- Encourage students to try combinations that add visual interest to the collage.

TEXTURE

Choosing to include texture as one of the important elements in your mural, along with shape and color, further widens options and can add originality and liveliness to the composition.

Texture in a collage can be created in several ways.

- Use an already textured paper like the inside of corrugated cardboard.
- Tear, rather than cut, one or more edges of a shape.
- Wrinkle and then flatten a particular paper.

Groups can experiment with creating texture and then adding textured areas to their images. Students assemble and glue together all of the basic shapes to create the images.

DETAILS

Details are very important to a work of art. They ensure that the images will be unique, quirky, and fun to look at. At this step in the process, imaginations can run wild!

Put up the work of each group. Ask the students to suggest what details could be added.

- Look for essential characteristic details and variety, like the different sizes and shapes of windows and leaves, or stripes and spots on fish and tigers.
- Lettering—"Fruit Stand" or "Shoe Store"—is inappropriate as a visual statement. An image of fruit or shoes in a window or on a sign is a more imaginative solution.

If your support is foam core, carefully tape the sheets together before the class begins the final organizing of the mural. It will then be possible to place images over the seams where desired.

Return the images to the groups so they can add their details. Leftover paper scraps sometimes suggest the shapes for details.

On the backs of two sheets of foam core, run three or four strips of one-inch wide masking tape horizontally across the seam. Then tape over the seam vertically.

VARIATIONS

There are two interesting variations of the basic paper collage mural that you may want to consider, especially with older students.

The shape of the support, rectangular or square, can be altered by cutting into the rectangle or by adding several shaped pieces to the top, bottom, or side edges of the rectangle.

- All cutting is done by the teacher using a sharp mat knife.
- The new pieces are taped to the rectangle and reinforced with additional tape.

To create a three-dimensional effect, small pieces of foam core can be cut in any shape, collaged, and glued to the support. This creates projections on the support. It is also possible to experiment with two layers by gluing one piece of foam core on top of another.

COMPOSING

After all of the images have been completed, the students must collectively refine and edit them as the last step before the final organization of the mural.

Lay out the support on the desk. Put all the collage images on the support in preparation for creating the final composition.

Looking at all the images laid out on the support, ask the students:

- What images does the mural still need?
- Which images need further details?

The entire class should participate. It may turn out that no revisions or additions are needed, but if they are, they should be made immediately so that the process can move ahead.

87. Composing, 6th grade

Organizing all of the images into one coherent composition is challenging.

·⚆· CHAPTER FIVE — APPROACHES TO COMPOSING A MURAL

When the class agrees that all of the images are complete, gather around the support to discuss how to organize the mural. There are a variety of ideas and questions to help the class put the pieces of the puzzle together.

With younger children, it is useful to begin by looking at the story or narrative.

- Set up the narrative in a visually logical sequence, from left to right or with a foreground, middleground, and background.

- There is a certain amount of intuition and trial and error involved in creating the final composition. Trust your eyes.

- Rearranging and moving one section may affect others. Take lots of time for class discussion. Take liberties. An unexpected placement—a figure in the sky, a fish on a bird's head—adds visual interest and originality.

- When all the images are composed, use push pins to hold them in place until the final gluing.

SPACE FOR THE TITLE

Titling the mural and signing it are important steps in the process. Students enjoy the collective job of choosing a title. It shifts their focus to other aspects (historical, scientific, literary) of the subject.

Space for the title and for signage must be integrated into the composition before the final gluing.

Brainstorm ideas for a title. You can use a colon to incorporate both a description and a variation. For example, "Fish and Goggles: The Undersea Mural," "The History of Money: From Cowrie Shells to ATM Cards."

As you compose, leave appropriate space for the length of the title and for the name of each student. Both are added after the final gluing. Typically, students sign the mural across the bottom, but other variations are certainly possible.

There are three possible techniques for adding your selected title in the space that has been set aside.

When it is time for titling and signing:

- The teacher selects the best *calligrapher* in the class to write the title with a permanent marker.

- Students cut out letter shapes from the assorted papers, arrange them in the proper order, and glue them to the support.

- Students cut out letters and/or words from magazines, arrange them, and glue to the support.

88. Assembling the collage, 6th grade

Installing is the step in the process that makes your art work a mural. It becomes both site specific and accessible to a large audience. In the case of the paper mural, the installation is relatively low tech, quick and easy.

Getting the mural up on the wall requires two pairs of hands, scissors, and a pencil. It is a very simple and satisfying task.

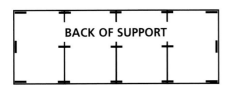

89. Placement of velcro strips

Your class is now ready to reap their public rewards.

Taking turns, each student signs the mural with a permanent marker.

FINAL GLUING

The final gluing should be done methodically.

- Do not attempt to glue down all of the images simultaneously.
- Work from left to right slowly and carefully.
- Each group, taking turns, glues down its own image.
- Neatness counts!

INSTALLING

To install your mural, we recommend self-adhesive velcro rather than double-sided tape because it is stronger, easier to work with, and less likely to damage the wall when removed.

Velcro comes in two strips, one *positive* and one *negative*. Each strip has an adhesive back covered with paper. When put together like a sandwich, the *positive* and *negative* velcro grab each other and stick together.

For a four-panel mural, you will need 60 inches of velcro.

- Without removing the paper backing, cut both halves of the velcro into 4-inch sections.
- Make the 4-inch sections into two-piece sandwiches of one positive and one negative piece.
- Remove the paper backing from one side of each sandwich.
- Adhere each sandwich to the back of the mural support across the seams and along the outer edges.

To install:

- Hold the mural up to the wall and situate it.
- With a pencil, lightly mark the position of each of the four corners.
- Remove all the remaining paper backing from the velcro strips.
- Using the corner pencil marks, position and adhere the mural to the wall.
- Firmly press down on all the areas of velcro stripping.

CHAPTER EIGHT – PLANNING THE CELEBRATION

*90. Paper on foam core,
    2nd grade*

The quality and lasting appeal of paper collage murals, even those made by the youngest students, often come as a surprise to the larger audience. One of the surprises is the fresh look of this fragile material. For years to come, your class mural will be seen by incoming students, parents, and staff as if it were brand new.

BUDGET:
MATERIALS AND TOOLS FOR THE PAPER COLLAGE MURAL

The cost of your paper collage mural depends primarily on the size you have selected. In all cases, it is important to use good quality materials and tools.

The prices listed here are based on one unit of an item. Prices may vary from location to location and year to year.

Foam core sheet, ¼-in. thick, 20 x 30-in. $6.00
   OR
Heavy colored paper, roll, 24 or 36-in. high $25.00
Chrome paper or other good quality colored paper, package,
   8 x 10-in. or 9 x 12-in. $5.00
Origami paper, patterned and metallic, package...$5.00
Folder with pocket or closed on three sides
   (one per student) ....$ .30
Glue stick, 10g $1.25
Scissors (Fiskars are recommended) $3.00
Velcro, 2 feet per foam core sheet ....$3.00 per foot

Pencils, erasers, markers, newspaper
Other possible papers: sandpaper, maps, phone book pages, wallpaper samples,
paint chip samples, corrugated paper

CHAPTER TEN

A DIFFERENT LOOK: THE FABRIC MURAL

THE MEDIUM OF fabric can be used in innovative and daring ways. For a fabric mural, the most practical choice is felt.

There are many advantages to the fabric mural. It can cover bad walls, its bright colors can be seen from a distance, and it is easy to install. Different grade levels can create a variety of images for the mural. The fabric mural is appropriate for grades 3 to 12 and can be completed in twelve to fifteen sessions.

91. Big shapes, fabric, junior high school (detail)

This chapter focuses on the creation of a fabric mural which we call the **BIG** shape mural that contains two or three very large fabric images. The **BIG** shape mural has one or two centerpiece images. Smaller images surround these **BIG** shapes to expand on the mural's primary ideas.

Another type of fabric mural is called a *grid* mural and contains a variety of *stories* or narratives set up in a grid pattern.

The fabric mural is a unique piece of artwork that can be the focal point for a school occasion, used as the narrative for your curriculum, or simply to beautify your school environment.

PREPARATION FOR THE FABRIC MURAL

Preparation and preplanning are important for the success of any large scale endeavor.

92. Subject: Native American cultures. Fabric, junior high school (detail)

Select the appropriate site, support color, and subject for your mural.

- Discuss with the custodian appropriate installation methods—rod sleeve or industrial velcro.
- Choose the background or support fabric color.
  - Choose a color in a mid-range. This will not limit the choices of the additional colors.
  - Yellow tends to fade and white quickly becomes dirty.
- Choose the most interesting and imaginative subject for your class. ☀ **CHAPTER THREE – THEMES**
- Make a small sample of a felt image glued onto another piece of felt.

DEFINING A MURAL

Define with your class the properties of murals in general:

- large scale
- site specific
- tells a story

Fabric murals in particular are made of cut pieces of fabric glued to a felt support.

- Show students your small sample.
- Pass around pieces of felt fabric.
  - Define texture.
  - Ask the class to describe the texture of the felt.

Show students the support.

From the very beginning, it helps students to see the scale of their project in order to understand the commitment and time that will be needed.

- Post the mural schedule. In order to keep up the momentum of the project, try to schedule mural classes at least twice a week. Discuss the time frame and schedule. Organize students into groups. ☀ **CHAPTER THREE – COLLABORATION**
- Have students sit with their groups
- Each group needs a folder which is closed on three sides. Folders should be labeled with the names of all the group members and are used to keep the work-in-progress.

Use brainstorming techniques to determine mural ideas.
☀ **CHAPTER THREE – BRAINSTORMING**

Although you have selected the subject for the class mural, students must provide their suggestions and ideas. The process of brainstorming serves to involve the whole class in an exchange of ideas and insures a sense of ownership of the mural.

After the major ideas have been selected, assemble a collection of appropriate pictures.
☀ **CHAPTER THREE – PICTURE FILE**

The setup of the space for students and their mural project is very important. Space is limited in many classrooms but there are a few basic strategies that will help to insure the comfort of students and teachers. Preparing tools and materials before distributing them will create an organized classroom tone.

Since students will work collaboratively in groups, they should discuss the various skills they bring to the project.

The fabric mural can be taught by breaking down the process into step-by-step, easy-to-understand procedures. By simplifying ideas, students will know exactly what to do and what is expected of them, and confusion will be reduced.

Practice lessons are an important part of the visual art process. All situations that involve learning and proficiency such as reading, mathematics, music, and sports require practice, practice, practice.

To insure that students understand all the sequential steps in making their fabric mural, they need to practice pattern-making, pinning, cutting, and gluing. During these lessons, students will be improving their skills and creating their own sample pieces.

CLASSROOM SET-UP

Divide students into groups.

- Combine desks so that one or two groups sit together.
- All the large pieces of fabric should be in one location at a supply table.
  - Scissors, glue, and pins are kept in separate plastic bins for easy distribution.
  - Desks are protected with newspaper or dropcloths.

Brainstorming can again be used here to determine the variety of skills needed for group work.

⟡ CHAPTER THREE – IDENTIFYING SKILLS

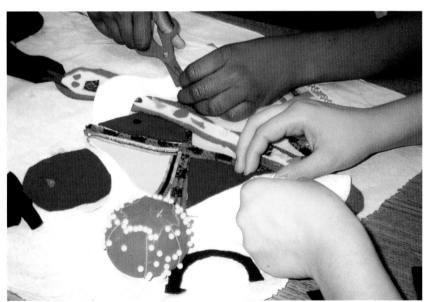

93. Pinning, junior high school

94. Gluing, high school

Patterns are an essential part of producing a fabric mural. They act as templates or guides in making all of the mural images. Students draw their images on heavy manila paper which is strong enough to withstand many corrections, pliable for easy pinning, and stiff enough for easy cutting. During pattern-making, students have the thinking time to correct their drawings and organize their group ideas. Students should not cut images directly from the fabric.

To become familiar with the process of a practice lesson, create a sample to show your class.

95. Drawing, 4th grade

PRACTICE PACKAGE

Organize a practice package for each of your students. This package consists of a small piece of manila paper, a small piece of felt, and one 9-inch piece of felt which will be used as a small support by each group. The same piece of felt and manila paper is used for all practice lessons.

PRACTICE PATTERN-MAKING

Distribute the practice package, a pencil, and dark markers to each group.

- Show the students your sample (manila paper with geometric shapes outlined in dark marker).
- Students review and draw geometric shapes on the board.
- Students draw one geometric shape on their manila paper and outline their shape in dark marker.

PRACTICE PINNING

Patterns need to be pinned to the felt fabric so that the pattern and the felt are held together for cutting.

Demonstrate pinning.

- Place the practice manila paper (with geometric shape) on the top of a small piece of felt.
- Gently fold both paper and fabric together. This positioning will make it easier for students to pin the manila paper and fabric.

96. Pinning, high school

- Insert the pin into the paper; go through the fabric and out the other side of the paper. Place pins about three inches apart.
- Distribute pin cushions to the class and explain how the pin cushion is used.
- Students place their geometric-shaped drawings on top of the piece of small felt fabric and practice pinning.
- Remind students not to pin across the marker line since this line is the place where they are going to cut.
- Students can help each other by one bending the manila paper and one pinning.

SCISSORS ETIQUETTE

Review with your class safe handling of scissors and exactly how to hold the scissors for cutting. We have found that many students need this instruction.

PRACTICE CUTTING FOR PATTERN-MAKING

The cutting of the manila drawings and the felt must be done very precisely in order to keep the integrity of the drawings. This skill is developed through practice.

Demonstrate the following cutting techniques on your pinned samples:
- Cut up to the dark marker line.
- Do not cut **OUT** the marker lines since the edge of the marker line determines the shape of the image.
- Keep turning the manila and fabric rather than turning hands and scissors.
- To change directions, stop, remove scissors, reposition the manila and fabric. Cut again.
- Students cut their practice manila and felt fabric on the desk, not in the air.

Slow, focused work is essential in this step.
- When students have finished cutting, return pins to pin cushion.
- Within each group, students are ready to organize their practice shapes.

PRACTICE COMPOSING

Composing the shapes is a challenging and creative step which requires collaborative planning. The groups have made three or more practice shapes and these are used for learning about composing.

⊙ CHAPTER TWO – COLOR AND COMPOSING

97. Fabric, 5th grade

Class artwork needs to be hung up, looked at, reviewed, and discussed. This gives students an opportunity to see their own group's work as part of the class's work, to see what other groups have accomplished, and to use art vocabulary to discuss the work.

Even if students know how to glue, fabric, especially felt, requires specific techniques. Excellent gluing skills are essential for a fabric mural. Neatness counts!

To practice composing, students will create minimurals.

- Each group places all of their individual practice felt shapes on their 9-inch felt support.
- Have two groups **PIN** their practice shapes on their 9-inch support and put up for viewing.
- Ask the following questions about arranging the shapes:
  - Which shape(s) can be the center of interest?
  - Which colors advance? Which colors recede into the background?
  - What happens to the flat surface when you try overlapping?
- Bring students up to the two practice pieces. Have them move the shapes around until a class consensus is reached about the most successful arrangements.
- After this discussion, groups work on composing their own shapes.
- Groups experiment with their shapes on their 9-inch felt support, and pin.

All minimurals are hung up for the entire class to see. Each piece is discussed. Which shapes move your eye around? Which colors advance? Which shapes are the center of interest?

Work is removed and stored in group folders.

PRACTICE GLUING

Use your own cut felt sample to demonstrate the gluing procedure.

- Put drop cloths or newspaper on the desks.
- Unpin shapes.
- One at a time, turn over each piece of cut felt.
- Run a narrow line or bead of white liquid glue around the perimeter of the shape.
- A glue X can be placed in the middle, for larger shapes.

98. Gluing, 4th grade

Review and make a list on the board of the skills students have learned from the pattern-making, cutting, composing, and gluing practice lessons. Students now have all the necessary technical skills to create their fabric mural, and they can begin to establish the relevant theme images.

- Turn over the felt and place it down on the support.
- **DO NOT APPLY PRESSURE**.
- Each group will remove their pins, put them in the pin cushion, and glue the practice shapes onto the 9-inch felt support.
- Place each glued work flat in a separate safe place for drying.
- When these minimurals are dry (about 1 hour), they can be put into the group folders.

You can ask students, "What skills did you learn from practicing? What did you learn that you did not know before?"

THEME IMAGES

Return and refer to the brainstorming list of ideas your class chose for their mural.

- Review each idea.
- Each group chooses only one idea on which to work.
- The picture file is used to find the appropriate theme images.
- Students can combine the picture file images or use the file as a jumping-off point to create drawings from their imaginations.

With their selected picture file images, students are ready to begin group pattern-making. Pattern-making requires drawing which is sometimes intimidating even for the teacher.

⁕ CHAPTER THREE – SHAPE LESSON

It gives students the confidence in being able to identify the geometric shapes in objects and replicate them in their drawings.

THE SHAPE LESSON

Teach the shape lesson.

- Distribute pencils and white practice paper.
- Each student practices the shape lesson using an image from the picture file.
- Put up all the work which should always be anonymous and discuss. For example, "What shapes were used in drawing A?" This type of questioning avoids judgmental comments and reinforces the concepts and techniques of the lesson.

After students have completed the shape lesson, they will be ready to undertake group drawing and pattern-making.

The selected images from the picture file give students a place to start. Drawing offers them a chance to experiment, discuss, revise, and see their ideas.

99. Drawing for pattern-making, high school

Details are very important to an artwork. When used they are engaging and fun to look at.

DRAWING FOR PATTERN-MAKING

For pattern-making, the shapes have to be **BIG**.

- Distribute pencils, manila paper, and dark markers.
- Each group produces one **LARGE** drawing.
- All students in a group collaborate on one drawing using one sheet of manila paper.
- Collaboration requires students to discuss the group's division of labor—who in the group will do what part of the drawing?
    - If the image is a school of fish, each student can do a variety of fishes.
    - If the image is one large fish, all group members can work on different parts of this fish.
- Students draw **BIG** by having their lines touch all the manila edges. ☀ **CHAPTER FIVE – DRAWING BIG**
- For the one or two centerpiece drawings, the manila paper can be taped together.
- All the **BIG SHAPE** drawings are put up and discussed in terms of their relevance to the mural theme.

DETAILS

Encourage students to look for essential details that will further define the characteristics of their image.
- For example, a bridge with cars and trucks, a window with curtains, coral under the sea, and variations on the bricks of buildings.
- Ask each group what details can be added to their drawings.
- Return the drawings so that each group can add their details.
- All details are drawn in pencil.
- Outline the **BIG** shape in dark marker.

All parts of the drawing are now ready to be translated into colored felt.

COLOR CHOICES

Color is magical! A fabric mural is full of wonderful colored shapes and details.

Students want to be guided in the how-to of selecting colors so they can be confident about their choices.

What colors will you choose and how will you choose them?

·☀· **CHAPTER TWO – COLOR**

- Cut small felt swatches of colors.
- Pin these onto the big support fabric for easy reference during the discussion of appropriate choices. Some ideas to consider:
  - Color is powerful and affects us all.
  - It can be brilliant, strong, or neutral.
  - It can change other colors by its position. See how a blue swatch looks with yellow or green near it.

CUTTING THE PATTERN

The texture of felt is uniform and flat, but overlapping shapes will give your mural shadow and depth. The fabric mural is constructed by layering and overlapping the cut shapes. The medium of felt lends itself to multilayered applications.

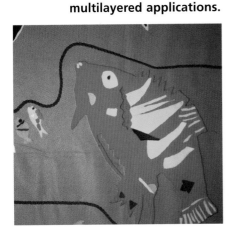

100. Color and overlapping, 5th grade

There are a variety of choices for combining and overlapping.
·☀· **CHAPTER NINE – ASSEMBLING AND GLUING**

One group at a time comes up to the supply table and chooses a dominant color for the first step of their pattern-cutting. You cut the fabric.

- Students return to their desks and pin their manila pattern-drawing onto their selected felt.
- Students slowly and carefully cut around their pattern on the marker line.
- Remove the pattern from the cut felt shape and put aside.

Students choose an assortment of colors for their details.

- Remind students to choose harmonious, complementary, or contrasting colors.
- Students cutout details and place the cut shapes on their big shape.

OVERLAPPING

During this process, the pattern or template will eventually be entirely cut up.

- Pin details onto the group's large shape.
- Students glue the details onto the large shape.

If you choose the rod and sleeve installation method, the sleeve must be prepared now to see the actual size of the support.

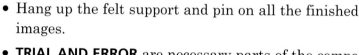 **CHAPTER TEN – INSTALLING**

PREPARING THE SLEEVE

To create the sleeve, measure, mark, and fold over four or five inches of felt. Pin and sew at the bottom edge of the fold. The sewing can be done by hand or machine, by you or older students.

COMPOSING

Now the fun begins! How will all the shapes in this puzzle fit together?

With all the images finished and ready to be assembled, students need to decide collectively how the images will be composed on the support. 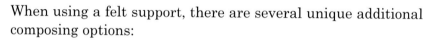 **CHAPTERS TWO AND FIVE – COMPOSING**

- Hang up the felt support and pin on all the finished images.
- **TRIAL AND ERROR** are necessary parts of the composing process.
- Pin and repin the images until all the images are unified.

When using a felt support, there are several unique additional composing options:

- Cut into the sides of the rectangle support.
- Cut into the bottom of the support to modify the rectangular shape.
- Place images near the bottom of the support to hang below the rectangle edge.

101. Composing, high school

FINAL GLUING

When composing is finished by class consensus, the final gluing can take place.

- Put the large felt support on a flat surface.
- Each large shape is gently placed down on the support and the top part pinned to hold it steady and in place.
- The bottom half is glued. If it is possible, let the bottom dry before the top is glued.
- The fabric mural should be left to dry, flat and in place, for a few hours or overnight if possible.
- Do not fold, bend, or roll the fabric. Folding creates creases and the glue cracks.

GRID FABRIC MURAL

The steps for making the grid fabric mural, up to COMPOSING, are the same as the steps for making the large shape fabric mural presented earlier in this chapter.

For the grid mural, each group creates a vignette. These visual stories will eventually be assembled in a grid format on a background support that fits your site. The vignettes, all of the same size, are arranged in horizontal and vertical rows.

Questions to ask when preparing for a grid fabric mural:

- What are the dimensions of your site?
- How many students are in your class?
  - We recommend, if possible, three students per group.
- Into how many vignette groups will you divide your class?
- What is the size of each vignette?

How to determine the size of each vignette:

- Use 9 or 12 vignettes for each grid fabric mural (with three students in each group).
- If your site is 48 x 48 inches, with 32 students there are 12 groups.
- This grid format will have three rows across and four rows down. Each vignette will be 12 x 16 inches.

All vignettes expand on the subject. Each one is self-contained. For example, for the subject of immigration:

- Each vignette depicts a different culture.
- Each story includes an environment. Where is the story taking place – a city, a village, under water?

102. Vignettes, 3rd grade

Each group will do all of their work on paper and felt on the size that you have chosen for the vignettes.

- Cut a manila paper sheet for each group that is the same vignette size you have determined.
- Students draw the image for their group vignette on this paper.
- Cut a felt vignette support for each group.

Each group chooses its felt color and translates the drawings into color.

COMPOSING FOR THE VIGNETTES OF THE GRID FABRIC MURAL

⚬ CHAPTERS TWO AND FIVE – COMPOSING

Place the large felt support on a flat surface.
On the fabric support, place the individual group vignettes. Arrange them in rows by:

- alternating complex and simple vignettes
- avoiding same-colored vignettes next to each other

GLUING THE VIGNETTES

When the final composing is completed, one group at a time comes up to the mural to glue their work, consecutively, left to right.

When this step is completed, the mural should be left in place without moving it for a few hours or overnight, if possible.

FINISHING TOUCHES

For both the **BIG** shape mural and grid mural, there are some finishing touches to consider.

- A variety of trim can be used as a frame around each vignette in the grid mural.
  - A piece of trim is cut to the size of the perimeter of each vignette.
  - This acts as a frame for each group's work and creates a finished look.
  - This framing also separates the stories from one another so the viewer is able to more easily see each individual piece.
- Trim can be applied to the entire perimeter of both types of fabric murals.
  - Leave excess trim on all the corners, fold under, and glue to back of support for a finished look.
- Glue is applied **TO THE FELT**, not to the trim.
  - Place the trim on the glue and gently press down.
  - Metallic trim is not advised since it is very difficult to adhere to felt.
  - Ribbon and ribbon-type trim can be used very successfully.
- If an area is not responding to glue, tack it down with a needle and thread.

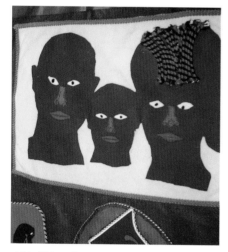

103. Trim, high school

104. Finishing touches, 5th grade

In consultation with the custodian, you have chosen whether to install your mural directly on the wall using industrial velcro or to hang the mural using the rod and sleeve method.

105. Fabric, high school

106. Rod and sleeve installation, high school

TITLE AND SIGNAGE

·ᯤ· CHAPTER EIGHT – TITLE AND SIGNAGE

Another option for titling a fabric mural — cut lettering out of felt and integrate into the composition.

INSTALLING – VELCRO METHOD

Velcro comes in two strips, one *positive* and one *negative*. Each strip has an adhesive back covered with paper. When put together like a sandwich, the *positive* and *negative* velcro grab each other and stick together.

- Place the fabric mural back side up on a flat surface.
- Without removing the paper backing, cut both halves of the velcro into sections to fit the length or width of the top of your mural.
- Make the sections into two-piece sandwiches of one positive and one negative piece.
- Remove the paper backing and run a continuous line across the back just below the top edge.
- Run a strip vertically along each outside edge beginning two inches from the top and, depending on the width of your mural, add several strips to the interior, one foot apart, parallel to the edge strips.
- Hold the mural up to the wall and lightly mark its final placement.
- Remove the paper backing and adhere to the wall.
- Make small 3-inch sandwiches of velcro to place along the lower sides and bottom to help the mural lay flat against the wall.

INSTALLING – ROD AND SLEEVE METHOD

Buy a wooden rod or dowel that is at least two inches longer than the mural sleeve.

- Use a large screw eye at each end of the rod to create a hanging system.
- The wooden rod or dowl is inserted into the mural sleeve.
- Install.

·ᯤ· CHAPTER EIGHT – PLANNING THE CELEBRATION

Fabric murals can tell stories about early evening in a Costa Rican rainforest or about a brightly colored abstract figure floating on multicolored shapes. While any narrative is possible, your class has found one voice and created a unique collective work of art that will be seen and appreciated within your school for years to come.

BUDGET
MATERIALS AND TOOLS FOR THE FABRIC MURAL

The cost of supplies for your fabric mural depends in part on the size you have selected. In all cases, it is important to use good quality materials and tools.

The prices listed here are based on one unit of an item except for the felt. Prices may vary from location to location and year to year.

FELT

The amount of felt listed here is based on a fabric mural support that is 48 inches x 72 inches, or 4 x 6 feet, and a cost of $8.00 per yard for 48-inch wide felt.

Support/background felt, 6 feet $48.00

1 yard each, red, blue, green, yellow felt...$32.00

½ yard each, black, brown, white, orange, turquoise, pink, purple felt $28.00

Small precut felt squares of any colors not available by the yard $20.00

Long straight pins with large head, package $5.00

Pin cushions $1.50

White glue, 4 ounces..$2.00

White glue, quart (for refilling) $8.00

Heavy manila paper, 14 x 17 inches or larger (3 sheets per group)...................................$ .50

Masking tape, roll...$1.50

Scissors (Fiskars are recommended) $3.00

Wooden rod/dowel, 2 inches longer than the mural sleeve $15.00

Pencils, erasers, markers, needle and thread

Assorted narrow and wide trim ribbon

ACKNOWLEDGEMENTS

This book was inspired by the thousands of children in New York City, in school and community settings, who have brought to mural-making their intelligence, creativity, patience, joy, curiosity and wonder. They have produced the beautiful works included in this book.

There are large numbers of people who have been participants either centrally or peripherally in our careers as muralists and educators; we appreciate and thank them all.

We wish to thank the organizations that through their sponsorship have enabled us to work in their programs with young people: ArtsConnection Inc., NYC; GOH Productions, NYC; Greenthumb, NYC Department of Parks and Recreation; Hestia Arts Collective, Northampton, MA; Music For Many Inc., Yorktown Heights, NY; St. Luke's-Roosevelt Hospital Center, NYC; Studio In A School Association, Inc., NYC; United Community Centers Inc., Brooklyn, NY; and Young Audiences/New York.

A small group of extraordinary people have not only understood our vision but have helped to make innovative projects possible through their advocacy: David Vas Nunes, Principal, CES 53, Bronx, NY; Lynn Kable, GOH Productions; Melvin Grizer, Executive Director, United Community Centers; Jane Weissman, former Director, Greenthumb (1984-98); and Dr. Mary Ann Castle, anthropologist, advocate and organizer extraordinaire who has created new opportunities for community partnerships throughout the country.

Education students at CUNY, through their concerns and questions about mural making made us aware of the need for a practical book on the process. Madeline Appell, Assistant Principal, High School of Fashion Industries and an author, emphatically encouraged us to pursue the idea of writing this book. The manuscript-in-progess was read by Jon Floyd, Dr. Barry Kaufman, Gail Kaufman, and R. Laura Reinitz, who we thank for their time and astute comments. Thank you to Amy Myer, contracts manager, for her time and advice in reviewing our contract.

The generosity of Toby Needler, Assistant Principal, Washington Irving High School, giving time, technology and friendship, turned out to be an essential ingredient in finishing this book.

Sondra Santoni did the impossible by taking a Luddite cut and paste manuscript and tirelessly making it clean and readable, over and over again.

Finally we gratefully thank our many friends whom we both neglected and leaned on for support during the process of writing this book.

Our special thanks to the Hubbards of Crystal Productions for their faith and trust in us. Their support came in the form of a rare blend of professionalism and patience.

CREDITS

1a-1b. East New York Women's Wall, acrylic paint on brick, 18 feet x 140 feet, 1993-95, Brooklyn, New York. Braun-Reinitz and Shicoff. United Community Centers, Inc.

2. History of Money: From Cowrie Shells to ATM cards, acrylic paint on plywood, 8 feet x 100 feet, 1995, New York City. Student collaboration: High School of Economics and Finance, High School of Fashion Industries and Landmark High School. ArtsConnection. Work in progress.

3. Our Neighborhood, acrylic paint on masonite, 4 feet x 8 feet, 1994. CES #53, Bronx, New York. ArtsConnection.

4. Sun Up, fabric, 4 feet x 5½ feet, 1998. P.S. 130, Brooklyn, New York. ArtsConnection.

5. Upside Down and Backyards, acrylic on brick, 6 feet x 100 feet, 1998. P.S. 205, Brooklyn, New York. Music for Many, Inc.

6. African Inspiration, acrylic paint on wood door, 7 feet x 3½ feet, 1993. Washington Irving High School, New York City. ArtsConnection.

7. The World Is One, acrylic paint on masonite, 4 feet x 24 feet, 1991. Studio In A School program at High School of Telecommunication Arts and Technology, Brooklyn, New York.

8. The History of Food, acrylic paint on plywood, 4 feet x 16 feet, 1995. CES #53, Bronx, New York. ArtsConnection.

9–27. Illustrations: Shicoff

28. Signs and Symbols (From Mali, West Africa to Brooklyn, New York), acrylic paint on brick, 10 feet x 55 feet, 1996, Brooklyn, New York. United Community Centers, Inc.

29. Dream on Jerome, acrylic paint on brick, 10 feet x 50 feet, 1993, Brooklyn, New York. United Community Centers, Inc.

30. Bounty, acrylic paint on plywood, 4 feet x 16 feet, 1998. Brooklyn, New York. United Community Centers, Inc.

31. Painting The World Green, acrylic paint on plywood, 4 feet x 20 feet, 1998. High School of Fashion Industries, New York City. ArtsConnection.

32. Toys Around the World, acrylic paint on plywood, 8 feet x 24 feet, 1996. CES #53, Bronx, New York. ArtsConnection.

33. *Violence In The City*, fabric, 6 feet x 4 feet, 1999. Martin Luther King Jr. High School, New York City. GOH Productions.

34. *The History of Women in Northampton: 1600-1980*, acrylic paint on cement, 24 feet x 134 feet, 1978-80. Northampton, Massachusetts. Hestia Art Collective.

35. *The Mantis Mural*, acrylic paint on brick, 30 feet x 38 feet, 1991. Brooklyn, New York. Braun-Reinitz.

36. *"Neptune" from Man/Woman and Mythology*, fabric, 7 feet x 4 feet, five panels of various sizes, 1996. Jacqueline Kennedy Onassis High School for International Careers, New York City. ArtsConnection.

37. CES #53, Bronx, New York. ArtsConnection.

38. Photo credit: Shicoff

39. Illustration: Shicoff

40-41. Photo credit & illustration: Braun-Reinitz

42. *The History of Food*, acrylic paint on plywood, 4 feet x 16 feet, 1995. CES #53, Bronx, New York. ArtsConnection.

43. Photo Credit: Braun-Reinitz

44. Illustration: Braun-Reinitz

45. *Contours in Color: Senior Mural*, acrylic paint on plywood, 8 feet x 24 feet, 1997. High School of Fashion Industries. ArtsConnection.

46. *We're Still Waiting*, acrylic paint on brick, 8 feet x 60 feet, 1994. Brooklyn, New York, United Community Centers, Inc.

47. Illustration: Braun-Reinitz

48. *Fata Morgana*, fabric, 20 feet x 6 feet, 1996. Stuyvesant High School, New York City. ArtsConnection.

49. *Painting the World Green*, acrylic paint on plywood, 4 feet x 20 feet, 1998. High School of Fashion Industries, New York City. ArtsConnection.

50. *Toys Around the World*, acrylic paint on plywood, 8 feet x 24 feet, 1996. CES #53, Bronx, New York. ArtsConnection.

51. Photo credit: Braun-Reinitz

52. *Safelife*, fabric, 6½ feet x 6 feet, 1998. Martin Luther King Jr. High School, New York City. GOH Productions.

53. Illustration: Braun-Reinitz

54. *The History of Food*, acrylic paint on plywood, 4 feet x 16 feet, 1995. CES #53, Bronx, New York. ArtsConnection.

55. *No Violence/Violencia No*, acrylic paint on shaped plywood, 4 feet x 40 feet, 1995. I.S. 302, Brooklyn, New York. United Community Centers, Inc.

56. *"Night" of Day and Night*, acrylic paint on plywood, 4 feet x 16 feet, 1999. P.S. 130, Brooklyn, New York. ArtsConnection.

57-58. *Toys Around the World*, acrylic paint on plywood, 8 feet x 24 feet, 1996. CES #53, Bronx, New York. ArtsConnection.

59. *Upside Down and Backyards*, acrylic on brick, 6 feet x 100 feet, 1998. P.S. 205, Brooklyn, New York. Music for Many, Inc.

60. *Families*, acrylic paint on plywood, 8 feet x 20 feet, 1996-97. P.S. 72, Brooklyn, New York. United Community Centers, Inc.

61. Illustration: Braun-Reinitz

62. Photo courtesy Crystal Productions.

63-65. Illustrations: Braun-Reinitz

66. *Pride*, acrylic paint on plywood, 8 feet x 16 feet, 1997. Savannah, Georgia. Metis Associates, New York City.

67. *Freedom Train: A Multi-Racial Journey*, acrylic paint on brick, 10 feet x 20 feet, 1992. Brooklyn, New York. United Community Centers, Inc.

68. *As Time Goes By: A History of East New York*, acrylic paint on brick, 13 feet x 100 feet, 1997. Brooklyn, New York. United Community Centers, Inc.

69. Illustration: Braun-Reinitz

70. *Celebrating 25 Years of Struggle*, acrylic paint on brick and cinder block, 8 feet x 110 feet, 1998. Brooklyn, New York. United Community Centers, Inc.

71. *Toys Around the World*, acrylic paint on plywood, 8 feet x 24 feet, 1996. CES #53, Bronx, New York. ArtsConnection.

72. *Past, Present and Future*, acrylic paint on plaster, 12 feet x 45 feet, 1994. Washington Irving High School, New York City. ArtsConnection.

73. *As Time Goes By: A History of East New York*, acrylic paint on brick, 13 feet x 100 feet, 1997. Brooklyn, New York. United Community Centers, Inc.

74-75. *History of Money: From Cowrie Shells to ATM cards*, acrylic paint on plywood, 8 feet x 100 feet, 1995, New York City. Student collaboration: High School of Economics and Finance, High School of Fashion Industries and Landmark High School. ArtsConnection.

76. *Pea Pods and Butterflies*, acrylic paint on brick, 10 feet x 80 feet, 2000. Brooklyn, New York. United Community Centers, Inc.

77. *History of Money: From Cowrie Shells to ATM cards*, acrylic paint on plywood, 8 feet x 100 feet, 1995, New York City. Student collaboration: High School of Economics and Finance, High School of Fashion Industries and Landmark High School. ArtsConnection.

78. *The History of Medicine*, acrylic paint on plywood, 4 feet x 8 feet, 1998. New York City, St. Luke's-Roosevelt Hospital Center.

79. P.S. 11 Doors, acrylic paint on plywood, 8 feet x 30 feet (total), 1994. New York City. P.S. 11.

80. *Four "Faces" of Our City*, paper on foam core, 2½ feet x 14 feet, 1998. P.S. 38, Brooklyn, New York. ArtsConnection.

81. *The Collage Project*, paper on mat board, various sizes, 2000. P.S. 107Q, Queens, New York. Young Audiences/New York.

82-84. Illustrations: Braun-Reinitz

85. *Four "Faces" of Our City*, paper on foam core, 2½ feet x 14 feet, 1998. P.S. 38, Brooklyn, New York. ArtsConnection.

86-88. *The Collage Project*, paper on mat board, various sizes, 2000. P.S. 107Q, Queens, New York. Young Audiences/New York.

89. Illustration: Braun-Reinitz

90. *Four "Faces" of Our City*, paper on foam core, 2½ feet x 14 feet, 1998. P.S. 38, Brooklyn, New York. ArtsConnection.

91. *Way Back When*, fabric, 6 feet x 3½ feet, 1999. P.S./I.S. 217M, Roosevelt Island, New York. Young Audiences/New York.

92-93. *The First Americans*, fabric, 6 feet x 3½ feet, 1999. P.S./I.S. 217M, Roosevelt Island, New York. Young Audiences/New York.

94. *Eat Right*, fabric, 6½ feet x 6 feet, 1999. Martin Luther King Jr. High School, New York City. GOH Productions.

95. Photo credit: Shicoff. P.S. 190, Brooklyn, New York. Sites for Students Program of New York City Board of Education.

96. *Fata Morgana*, fabric, 20 feet x 6 feet, 1996. Stuyvesant High School, New York City. ArtsConnection.

97. *Spotted Fish and Plaid Turtles*, fabric, 6 feet x 19 feet, 1999. P.S. 38, Brooklyn, New York. ArtsConnection.

98. *Sun Up*, fabric, 4 feet x 6 feet, 1998. P.S. 130, Brooklyn, New York. ArtsConnection.

99. *Safelife*, fabric, 6½ feet x 6 feet, 1998. Martin Luther King Jr. High School, New York City. GOH Productions.

100. *Spotted Fish and Plaid Turtles*, fabric, 6 feet x 19 feet, 1999. P.S. 38, Brooklyn, New York. ArtsConnection.

101. *"Diana" from Man/Woman and Mythology*, fabric, five panels of various sizes, 1996. Jacqueline Kennedy Onassis High School for International Careers, New York City. ArtsConnection.

102. *Stories*, fabric, 3 feet x 5 feet, 1998. P.S. 85, Queens, New York. ArtsConnection.

103. *Safelife*, fabric, 6½ feet x 6 feet, 1998. Martin Luther King Jr. High School, New York City. GOH Productions.

104. *Spotted Fish and Plaid Turtles*, fabric, 6 feet x 19 feet, 1999. P.S. 38, Brooklyn, New York. ArtsConnection.

105. *"Aboriginal Night and Day" from Man/Woman and Mythology*, fabric, five panels of various sizes, 1996. Jacqueline Kennedy Onassis High School for International Careers, New York City. ArtsConnection.

106. *Fata Morgana*, fabric, 20 feet x 6 feet, 1996. Stuyvesant High School, New York City. ArtsConnection.